Improving
Organizational
Performance

SAGE HUMAN SERVICES GUIDES

A series of books edited by ARMAND LAUFFER and CHARLES D. GARVIN. Published in cooperation with the University of Michigan School of Social Work and other organizations.

Improving Organizational Performance

A Practical Guidebook for
the Human Services Field

Gary V. Sluyter

SHSG SAGE HUMAN SERVICES GUIDES 74

*Published in cooperation with the University
of Michigan School of Social Work*

SAGE Publications
International Educational and Professional Publisher
Thousand Oaks   London   New Delhi

For information:

SAGE Publications, Inc.
2455 Teller Road
Thousand Oaks, California 91320
E-mail: order@sagepub.com

SAGE Publications Ltd.
6 Bonhill Street
London EC2A 4PU
United Kingdom

SAGE Publications India Pvt. Ltd.
M-32 Market
Greater Kailash I
New Delhi 110 048 India

Printed in the United States of America

Library of Congress Cataloging-in-Publication Data

Sluyter, Gary V.
    Improving organizational performance: A practical guidebook for the human services field / by Gary V. Sluyter.
        p.   cm.—(Sage human services guides ; v. 74)
    Includes bibliographical references and index.
    ISBN 0-7619-0750-5 (cloth: acid-free).—ISBN 0-7619-0751-3 (pbk. : acid-free)
    1. Human services—Evaluation. 2. Organizational effectiveness.   I. Title. II. Series.
    HV40.S595 1998
    361'.0068'4—dc21   97-21203

98 99 00 01 02 03 10 9 8 7 6 5 4 3 2 1

Acquiring Editor:	Jim Nageotte
Editorial Assistant:	Kathleen Derby
Production Editor:	Michele Lingre
Production Assistant:	Karen Wiley
Typesetter/Designer:	Yang-hee Syn Maresca
Indexer:	Teri Greenberg
Cover Designer:	Candice Harman
Print Buyer:	Anna Chin

To all the organizations I have worked for or with
over the years . . .
I am grateful for what you have taught
and I have learned.

TABLE OF CONTENTS

FOREWORD

The concept of *organization* in and of itself implies a gathering together of entities or elements for a common purpose. We use the term in myriad situations and frequently as an analogy to underscore or explain or describe a coming together of some sort. To improve this thing we call an organization, in whatever form it takes, we must understand it and see where it is now and where we collectively would like it to be. Then we set about the identification of processes that are aimed at getting us to the desired outcome —from where it is now to where we want it to be. Inevitably, there is widespread consensus that that outcome is customer satisfaction because that satisfaction is the *sine qua non* of survival and we all share familiarity with the lengths to which we go to survive.

With the advent of acceptance of the teachings of W. Edwards Deming, Joseph Juran, Philip Crosby, Peter Senge, Margaret Wheatley, and Russell Ackoff, among many others, we have come to understand that the days of linear thinking—simple cause and effect—got us into a particularly interesting bind. As we solved today's problems, we created tomorrow's. As we rid ourselves of malicious bacteria, we celebrate that moment; as we celebrate, the organism, always adapting, breeds anew to adjust to our tampering. The very antidote that alleviates or arrests or even cures thus is the same that creates an environment in which new challenges surface.

My brilliant and highly esteemed colleague, Gary Sluyter, who also is a warm and caring friend, has taken the concept of continuous improvement and synthesized an essential wholeness perspective. Through examples and descriptions of organizational cultures and habits, he helps us down the path of understanding how people in organizations learn by seeing themselves as a whole unit rather than distinct and separate parts.

He demonstrates in some very practical hands-on ways that to improve, we must have mutual understanding of what improvement would really look like, going beyond the wordsmithing of mission and vision statements.

After reading *Improving Organizational Performance,* you might see the concepts of focus, departments, units, productivity, culture, profit, integration, customer, empowerment, change, strategic planning, and leadership, among others, in a whole new light. I have walked down many paths with Gary Sluyter over the years. I trust you will enjoy and benefit greatly from your walk down this path with him.

Myrna J. Casebolt
Madison, Wisconsin

INTRODUCTION

The world seems to be radically different than it was when I began my career in the early 1960s. That was an exciting time for people interested in the helping professions, a time marked by abundant resources, an experimental attitude, and eternal optimism about the effectiveness of our human service interventions.

Today, it seems that we have lost much of the excitement of that once-enthusiastic vision about the value of our work in this field. Budgets are tight, worker burnout and turnover are high, and taxpayers are pessimistic about the value of what we do. This does not create a very rewarding or motivating organizational climate and leads to mediocre and often substandard services.

Hasenfeld and English (1978) characterized this climate as one of "consumer revolt" and identified four major themes in a growing public protest: (a) failure of human service organizations to respond to client needs, (b) lack of organizational effectiveness, (c) insensitivity to individual needs and characteristics, and (d) poor and inefficient management (p. 3).

Martin and Kettner (1996) echoed similar concerns a decade and a half later, suggesting that current moves by funding agencies to scrutinize human service organizations seem to be related to "a general dissatisfaction with their *performance* rather than to a general repudiation of their intrinsic or moral worth" (p. 2). In some ways, that is good news, at least if one believes that the performance of human services organizations *can* be improved.

This book is about the nature of performance in such organizations. It contains some ideas about how to improve that performance, especially in our current environment. The lessons herein are derived from my own experiences, some 30 years of working in and around a wide variety of human service organizations, and they come from a deeply optimistic view that we *can* get better at what we do.

During those three decades, I worked as a summer day camp counselor for people with disabilities, recreational therapist for emotionally disturbed children, probation counselor with delinquent youth, caseworker, orphanage director, public health adviser, grant administrator, state institutional superintendent, state program director, teacher, trainer, and organizational consultant. My purpose here is to try to pull together and integrate some of the things I have learned through those experiences, providing a kind of field guide for use by practitioners interested in improving the performance of their organizations. The external climate in which we now must function is exerting an increasing amount of pressure for us to demonstrate both the effectiveness and the efficiency of our organizations. I hope that this book will be a useful and practical guide for organizational leaders trying to stay ahead of that power curve.

Hasenfeld and English (1978) describe human service organizations as having three major roles: (a) *socialization of society's members,* as in schools and youth-serving agencies; (b) *social control agents,* such as correctional institutions and law enforcement agencies; and (c) *social integration agents,* such as mental health agencies. Furthermore, these various types of organizations provide a wide variety of either "people processing" or "people changing" services (pp. 2-3).

Although the bulk of my experience has been with mental health or behavioral health care organizations, clearly in the social integration and people changing categories, the ideas to be discussed are equally applicable to other organizations in the human services, health care, or educational arenas, in both the public and private sectors. Accordingly, I will use terminology, case examples, and concepts from a variety of settings. I hope this approach will facilitate communication and ease of application.

A definition for the term "performance improvement" will be developed in the first chapter of the book. In general, it refers to the organization's systematic efforts to improve the quality of services for its customers or consumers continuously, as well as the quality of work life for its employees. People depend on us to provide them with the best services we can offer. If we are to remain a vital force in helping to make a better world, the work of improving the performance of our human service organizations cannot wait.

GVS
St. Louis, Missouri
February 7, 1997

REFERENCES

Hasenfeld, Y., & English, R. A. (Eds.). (1978). *Human service organizations: A book of readings*. Ann Arbor: University of Michigan Press.

Martin, L. L., & Kettner, P. M. (1996). *Measuring the performance of human service programs*. Thousand Oaks, CA: Sage

Chapter 1

WHY PERFORMANCE IMPROVEMENT?

Anne Fairweather's first day as Executive Director of the Centerville Mental Health Center was a memorable one. After arriving at her office, she was reading over some deficiency reports from the Joint Commission on Accreditation of Healthcare Organizations (JCAHO) when she received an urgent message that a consumer was holding an employee hostage in the lunchroom. She barely got to the door when her secretary advised her that there was a news reporter on the line asking about a report about some drugs missing from one of the group homes.

Anne waved off the call and headed toward the lunchroom, only to run into two of her department heads arguing bitterly about whose job it was to perform a task. When she arrived at the lunchroom, she encountered an employee who was escorting a patient outside. She asked the employee what had happened and was told simply, "Oh, it was just a misunderstanding." As they walked outside, Anne noticed that the patient appeared to have a swollen eye and was holding her arm at a funny angle.

Returning to her office, Anne was accosted by a woman who identified herself as a parent of one of the residents. The woman was complaining bitterly that the Center had lost her daughter's new coat. Anne promised to look into the problem and returned to her office, only to encounter a TV news crew wanting to interview her about "alleged improprieties" in the Center's fiscal affairs.

LEARNING OBJECTIVES

- To introduce and define the concept of "organizational performance"
- To link the study of organizational performance with that of Total Quality Management

- To introduce the concept of customers and their role in improving performance
- To introduce and describe a model for organizational performance

As a species, humankind, more than any other of Earth's creatures, seems to be fascinated with the study of individual and group performance. In all fields of human endeavor, whether physical endurance, the arts, or technology, we always seem to be trying to improve on some previous standard. The events of the Olympic Games are, perhaps, one of humankind's most elegant reflections of its eternal quest for setting performance standards and continuously trying to exceed them.

Because the great majority of goods and services we rely on every day are produced through organizations, we are also vitally interested in organizational performance, applying a great variety of individual and group measures to monitor that performance. Like individual performance, the work of organizations, including those that provide vital human services, can be assessed in terms of success or failure.

Many of the issues confronting Anne on her first day of work concerned the performance of her organization, and all reflected some degree of organizational failure. Accreditation deficiencies, the lunchroom disturbance, missing drugs, internal squabbles, possible client abuse, parent complaints, and allegations of fiscal impropriety all represent issues that will affect Anne's success or failure as the organization's leader. Although they are not as evident, there are likely as many things going right at Centerville as there are things going wrong.

Questions of performance in human services organizations and how to achieve it are the central issues of this book. As we shall see, organizational performance is a complex and far from agreed-upon concept, yet one that is becoming critical for organizational survival.

ORGANIZATIONAL
PERFORMANCE DEFINED

In my seminars on quality management in mental health, I often ask the question, "What is the best psychiatric hospital in the United States?" I get a variety of answers that inevitably include the Menninger Clinic in Topeka, Kansas, and Johns Hopkins Hospital in Baltimore, among others.

I then ask, "How do you know?" "What sets these organizations apart from others?" and "What are the factors that make them the best?" This exercise then becomes a prelude to a listing of those factors. The lists vary but usually include such things as *accessibility, customer-friendly processes, high-quality staff,* and *good outcomes.* I emphasize the fact that none of these successful facilities became successful by chance. In all cases, the leadership of the organization had to have created a vision of excellence and a plan for getting there.

I also ask seminar participants to rate their organizations on two factors, *quality of services for clients* and *quality of work life for employees.* Each of these factors is rated on a five-point scale, from 1 = *Terrible* to 5 = *Excellent.* After collecting participants' anonymous responses, I create a frequency diagram on a flip chart and display the results for all to see.

I have collected this information from dozens of mental health organizations in eight states, and I get curiously similar results each time. Although the mean scores and standard deviations differ slightly, the picture looks like Figure 1.1. I then ask people what they make of the data and get several fairly standard answers.

"Well, we certainly can improve what we are doing."

"Looks like we're doing better for our clients than we are for ourselves."

"I guess we are about as good (or as bad) as our colleagues in other organizations."

"I think it speaks well of the employees that we are doing as well as we are for our clients in spite of our working conditions."

"I wonder, if we improved the quality of our work life, would the quality of our services improve as well?"

This then leads to a generally fruitful discussion about some of the barriers to improvement. More often than not, a lack of resources is listed as one of the immediate barriers. In addition, however, participants acknowledge that the organization itself and the way it is managed often gets in the way of doing the best job possible.

During these introductory or warm-up exercises, I also ask people to reveal how long they have worked at their respective jobs, either in the current organization or in similar ones. We then group the responses and create another frequency diagram on the flip chart. In this case, the shape of the diagram varies considerably from organization to organization, with a range of experience from 1 day to 30 years.

I then suggest that tenure is a kind of proxy for competence (although not always) and do a cumulative total of years of experience. For groups of 30-50 participants, we often end up with between 200 to 300 years of cumulative experience. I then invite the participants to reflect on the significance of having several hundred years of cumulative experience or

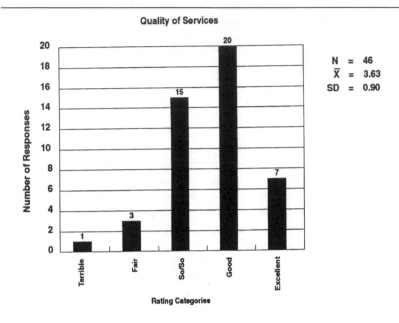

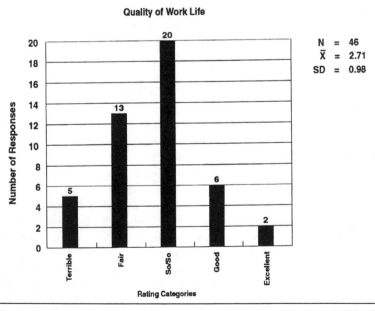

Figure 1.1. *Ratings by Program Participants of Quality of Services and Quality of Work Life*

"knowledge power" in the room, and to wonder what the total would be for the whole organization.

Finally, I ask people to give me an estimate of the percentage of that knowledge power that is being used within their organization on a daily basis: "To what extent do you feel that you can apply the full weight of your experience and knowledge to help improve the quality of services and quality of work life? How often does the organization ask for your opinions about how to do things? How free do you feel to make suggestions and share your ideas about how to make things better?"

At this point, some nervous laughter breaks out throughout the room. People sink down in their seats in dread anticipation of being called on for an answer. I tell them that it is somewhat rhetorical and theoretical, as I don't have any useful measures to get at the answer. I also tell them, however, that when I ask this question for real, and when people are candid with me, the general response is between 20% and 30%!

I then use the analogy of an eight-cylinder, supercharged, high-performance, 400-horsepower automobile engine from which someone has removed two spark plugs. Even with all of its potential power, that engine simply cannot perform effectively or efficiently in that condition.

Organizations often are very much like that engine. They have tremendous potential for performance but encounter organizational barriers that rob them of that potential. As a result, they only partially use the tremendous human resources at their disposal. The net result is substandard, mediocre, and lackluster services for the people we serve and less than optimal work environments for ourselves.

Unfortunately, our traditional approach to monitoring and improving the performance of human service organizations relies to a great extent on external judgments, made by some more or less independent licensing or accrediting body. Entities such as state licensing bureaus, accreditation organizations, and Medicaid certification units play a great role in how we define and measure our overall performance. This approach, though perhaps necessary, may not be sufficient.

These external "quality assurance" or "inspection" systems measure performance on the basis of published standards or criteria that have been developed through expert panels and other input. Failure of the organization to comply with these standards or requirements results in deficiency reports and can lead to certain sanctions against the organization, such as loss of accreditation, funding freezes, and negative publicity.

Although external standards can be useful yardsticks by which leaders can assess the performance of their organizations, they suffer from a number of limitations.

1. This approach causes the organization to become externally focused and dependent on others for defining and ultimately managing the quality of its services.
2. Performance begins to be viewed within a compliance or punitive framework.
3. External performance monitoring systems may focus more on professional standards of care or service rather than on the needs of agency customers.
4. Deficiency reports are often handled as ends in themselves instead of as means for improving internal systems that may be causing the problems.

During my seminars, I often ask participants to describe what happens to the organization when they know that the external surveyors are likely due for a site visit. Invariably, the response is immediate and universal. People say things like, "The place goes bananas!" "Everyone scurries around trying to get things in order at the last minute" "It is a really crazy time . . . nobody gets any other work done!"

I then ask, "Well, what happens when the survey is over and the surveyors are gone?" Again, immediate and consistent responses, such as, "Whew! We all breathe a great collective sigh of relief . . . and then go right back to doing things like we always did before the surveyors came around!"

If our traditional approaches to organizational performance have severe limitations, what are our alternatives? What can we tell Anne Fairweather that will help her deal with the kinds of problems she encountered on her first day of work? How can we become more proactive in our efforts to improve our organizations? Those are some of the questions I hope to answer in this book. Before we get directly into that, however, I need to lay a little more foundation.

ENTER QUALITY MANAGEMENT

One alternative approach to evaluating organizational performance, and a basic building block for the discussion to follow, is a management philosophy sometimes referred to as *Total Quality Management (TQM)* or *Continuous Quality Improvement (CQI)*. I particularly like this approach because it enables us to integrate our traditional reliance on external monitoring with a more internally focused and proactive performance improvement system.

Others (Walton, 1986) have traced the history of the quality management movement from its introduction in Japan in the 1950s to its later rediscovery by American industry, so I will not try to redo that work.

Martin (1993), a pioneer in the application of quality principles to the human services field, provides a very readable and succinct historical review of the quality management movement and suggests that it is based on the ideas of four individuals: W. Edwards Deming, Joseph Juran, Phil Crosby, and Armand Feigenbaum. In developing my own understanding of quality management, I have been most influenced by Deming and Juran, both of whose lectures I have had the privilege of attending.

Although quality management concepts have been applied to manufacturing environments for many years, it appears that their application to general health care, mental health, government, education, and the human services did not begin to emerge until late in the 1990s. Leaders of human service organizations are just now beginning to appreciate the power of this philosophy to help us improve the performance of our agencies.

I have seen dozens of definitions of TQM and CQI. Most have several elements in common. I define it as "a leadership philosophy that helps organizations identify and continuously reach quality outcomes for all of their customers through the application of systems thinking, analytic techniques, and the involvement of everyone." The Shawnee Hills Mental Health Center in Charleston, West Virginia, uses a much more parsimonious definition: "Quality is exceeding your expectations!" (Sluyter & Barnette, 1995, p. 280).

A helpful framework for understanding the common elements of various quality management approaches is provided in a 1991 report by the U.S. Government Accounting Office (USGAO, 1991). At the request of a U.S. congressman, the GAO studied 22 American corporations that had applied for the Malcolm Baldrige National Quality Award, to determine commonalties of approach and identified five important elements that were common to each of the organizations that had adopted quality management philosophies.

1. *Strong Quality Leadership:* The management of the organization gives direction, impetus, and energy to the management of performance by taking personal responsibility for quality issues and by continuously communicating and reinforcing its approach throughout the organization.

2. *Customer-Driven:* The organization begins by defining who its customers are (beneficiaries, employees, and stakeholders), determining what they want or expect from the organization, and then deciding how organizational performance will be defined and measured, based on those expectations.

3. *Continuous Improvement:* The organization uses a "systems approach" to develop structures and methods for continuously evaluating and improving the ways it designs and delivers its services.

4. *Action Based on Facts, Data, and Analysis:* The organizational culture moves away from a "shoot-from-the-hip" approach to problem solving to one that uses data and information effectively in decision making at all levels.

5. *Employee Involvement:* Employees are valued as the organization's most important resource, are treated well, and are involved routinely and deeply in important decisions affecting organizational performance. Individual and team creativity and suggestions are actively encouraged and consistently rewarded.

The Baldrige Award itself uses a framework that includes the following seven elements to assess organizational quality: Leadership, Strategic Planning, Customer and Market Focus, Information and Analysis, Human Resource Development and Management, Process Management, and Business Results (Bemowski, 1996).

These ideas about the management of quality, including these basic elements of the Baldrige Award, are central to the organizational performance model to follow and are based on assumptions that are quite different from traditional approaches. There are at least ten basic assumptions underlying this management or leadership philosophy.

1. Organizational performance must be driven by strong and committed leadership.

2. The organization's customers are the center of everything the organization does.

3. All work is a process or part of a process. To improve or change performance involves changes to those processes. Further, only management can change the processes (Deming, 1986).

4. Performance or quality failures are primarily the result of faulty processes or work systems and not faulty employees.

5. Employee mistakes and errors are opportunities for learning and prevention of future failures.

6. The management of quality extends beyond inspection or quality assurance and includes both quality planning and quality improvement (Juran, 1989).

7. The approach to improving quality of work must be ongoing and continuous.

8. Decisions are made on the basis of facts, data, and analysis and not guesswork.

9. Improved organizational performance is best achieved by involving all employees in the process.

10. Services are designed and delivered on the basis of a blend of both customer and professional inputs.

To determine the extent to which your organization reflects traditional or quality management philosophies, complete the *Organizational Assessment Scale* at the end of the chapter.

One of the basic tenets of this "new" philosophy suggests that organizational performance must be measured from the point of view of all the customers or stakeholders that benefit from its products or services, also called "constituencies" (Daft, 1992, p. 53). For a human services organization, performance might be judged in terms of several customer groups, including consumers and their families, the employees, the community, and funding agencies. External accreditation or licensing bodies, then, become only one of the definers of performance quality for the organization. Based on this view, I define organizational performance as "the organization's overall effectiveness in meeting the identified needs of each of its constituent groups through systematic efforts that continuously improve its ability to address those needs effectively."

To be effective as an administrator of the Centerville Mental Health Center, then, Anne must define her organization's success in terms of the degree it is able to satisfy the demands of those various constituencies. This means that she will have to be able to address the external accreditation deficiency reports and use that information to improve her organization's systems, respond to questions from the press, help her warring employees learn to treat one another like customers, understand and address the causes of client abuse while balancing the legitimate interests of her employees and clients, address the demands of parents in appropriate ways, and be accountable to her stakeholders and the public for her stewardship of the agency's resources.

Furthermore, she must be able to articulate the Center's purpose or mission clearly, envision a direction for its future, set goals, establish a framework or structure for performance, develop performance measures based on the needs of the various constituencies, and devise a way of systematically collecting data from those measures that can be used for continuously improving the organization's effectiveness, while involving all of her employees. This process is depicted in Figure 1.2 and forms the basic conceptual framework that will serve as the foundation for the discussion to follow. As illustrated in this model, performance improvement is driven by leadership that accepts the basic responsibility for organizational performance improvement and makes a serious commitment to the process. The first step is to establish governing ideas for the organization (mission, vision, and values) and to set a strategic direction. That process begins with the identification of all the organization's customers and stakeholders, as well as their requirements. This, in turn,

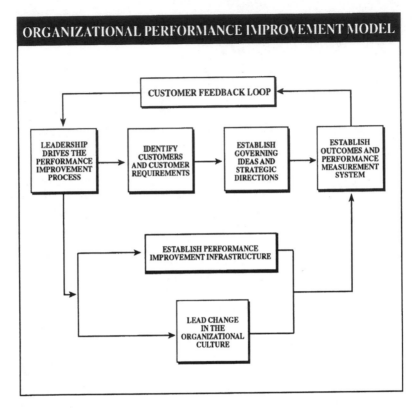

Figure 1.2. *Organizational Performance Improvement Model*

provides data for the strategic planning process. Based on an understanding of customer requirements, the key organizational performance outcomes and measurement system are established. Finally, leadership leads necessary changes in the organizational culture, and makes sure that the infrastructure is in place to support performance improvement efforts.

We will examine each component of this model in the chapters to follow. Chapters 2 and 3 focus on basic and vital customer questions: "Who are they and what do they need from us?" Chapter 4 outlines an approach to developing governing ideas and strategic plans. It is followed by an examination of change in the organizational culture in Chapter 5. In Chapter 6, we look at the issue of measuring performance; notes on developing a supportive infrastructure follow in Chapter 7.

Chapter 8 provides an integrating case study that follows a performance improvement team as it works to resolve a serious absenteeism problem at Central State Hospital. Finally, in Chapter 9, we provide an annotated bibliography and other helpful performance improvement resources, including a "performance improvement tool kit." Let us begin (as we always should) with our customers.

REFERENCES

Bemowski, K. (1996). Baldrige Award celebrates its 10th birthday with a new look. *Quality Progress, 29*(12), 49-54.

Daft, R.L. (1992). *Organizational theory and design*. New York: West.

Deming, W. W. (1986). *Out of the crisis*. Cambridge: Massachusetts Institute of Technology, Center for Advanced Engineering Technology.

Juran, J. M. (1989). *Juran on leadership for quality: An executive handbook*. New York: Free Press.

Martin, L. L. (1993). *Total Quality Management in human service organizations*. Newbury Park, CA: Sage.

Sluyter, G. V., & Barnette, J. E. (1995). Application of Total Quality Management to mental health: A benchmark case study. *The Journal of Mental Health Administration, 22*(3), 278-285.

U.S. Government Accounting Office. (1991). *Management practices: U.S. companies improve performance through quality efforts* (GAO/NSIAD-91-190). Washington, DC: Author.

Walton, M. (1986). *The Deming management method*. New York: Perigee Books.

BOX 1.1. *Organizational Assessment Scale*

Instructions: Below are listed ten items that describe various aspects of how organizations operate. Please read each item and score it on the basis of how descriptive it is of *your organization.* Use the following scale:

Not at All Descriptive	Slightly Descriptive	Moderately Descriptive	Generally Descriptive	Highly Descriptive
1	2	3	4	5

QUESTIONS	RATINGS (Circle your choice for each)
1. The leadership of my organization has clearly accepted responsibility for organizational quality and performance. Organizational leaders are personally involved in efforts to improve what we do, and they consistently demonstrate their commitment	1 2 3 4 5
2. We try to base our organizational processes, plans, and decisions on a clear understanding of who our customers and stakeholders are and what they need from us.	1 2 3 4 5
3. We view all work as a process and understand that performance improvement involves a deep understanding of those processes.	1 2 3 4 5
4. We understand that quality failures are most often the result of faulty systems or processes and not faulty employees. Our approach to improvement focuses more on improving systems and less on punishing employees for their mistakes.	1 2 3 4 5
5. The management of quality in our organization extends beyond inspection and quality control and includes both quality planning quality improvement efforts.	1 2 3 4 5
6. We approach performance goals through continuous improvement over extended time periods, rather than seeking short-term breakthroughs or crisis management.	1 2 3 4 5
7. We try to make organizational decisions on the basis of facts, data, and analysis rather than random, trial and error efforts.	1 2 3 4 5
8. We believe that organizational performance is best achieved by involving all employees, and we have specific systems for including them in the decision-making process (e.g., improvement teams).	1 2 3 4 5
9. We design and deliver our client services on the basis of a blend of customer input and the judgments of our professional practitioners.	1 2 3 4 5
10. We believe that employee mistakes and errors are opportunities from which to learn and prevent future failures.	1 2 3 4 5

Organizational Assessment Scale Scoring Key

1. Add up scores for the 10 items and
   write the total here (maximum 50 points): _____

2. Multiply score by 2 to get a percentage score and
   write the result here: _____%

3. Interpret results as shown below.

Score of 0 to 25%:   Your organization's management style does not yet reflect the assumptions and principles of quality improvement presented here. Encourage leadership to evaluate the potential benefits of a quality management approach and make a commitment to obtain the training and help needed to adopt it.

Score of 25 to 50%:   Your organization is beginning to practice some of the quality improvement principles but has not yet reached a sustained and consistent effort. Assess weak areas, develop specific improvement targets, and seek additional training for staff in quality improvement philosophy and techniques.

Score of 50 to 75%:   Your organization has made a good start toward quality management principles. Assess weak areas and develop specific improvement targets. Seek other organizations with which to benchmark.

Score of 75 to 100%:   Your organization is well on its way to becoming a world-class service agency. Evaluate any weak areas, develop specific targets, and stay the course.

Chapter 2

WHO ARE OUR CUSTOMERS?

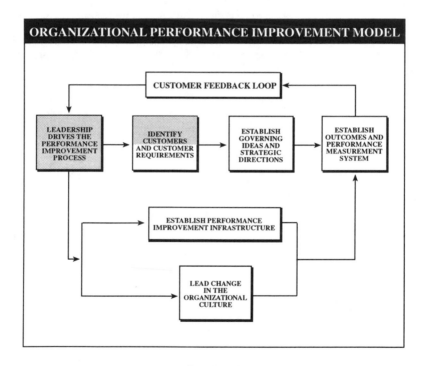

ORGANIZATIONAL PERFORMANCE IMPROVEMENT MODEL

CUSTOMER FEEDBACK LOOP

LEADERSHIP DRIVES THE PERFORMANCE IMPROVEMENT PROCESS

IDENTIFY CUSTOMERS AND CUSTOMER REQUIREMENTS

ESTABLISH GOVERNING IDEAS AND STRATEGIC DIRECTIONS

ESTABLISH OUTCOMES AND PERFORMANCE MEASUREMENT SYSTEM

ESTABLISH PERFORMANCE IMPROVEMENT INFRASTRUCTURE

LEAD CHANGE IN THE ORGANIZATIONAL CULTURE

CHAPTER 2
WHO ARE OUR CUSTOMERS?

ST. LUKE'S COMMUNITY HOSPITAL
AND HEALTH CARE CENTER

It was late on a Friday afternoon as Sister Mary Veronica Schultz, MHA, sat at her desk rubbing her temples and thinking to herself, "What a week!" Ever since the mother house had appointed her as administrator of the St. Luke's Community Hospital and Health Care

Center, she had been feeling a little pressured. Not that she wasn't up to the task. As an experienced hospital administrator, just back from a teaching sabbatical, she was quite familiar with the everyday challenges of the job. But this past week!

In her mind's eye, she reviewed the issues that had come across her desk, beginning early on Monday morning.

1. A letter from a patient's family complaining about problems with the care given to the family member by the hospital.
2. A phone call from the president of the local chamber of commerce expressing serious concerns about the hospital's expansion plans.
3. A petition from the hospital's salaried employees complaining about the new sick leave policy.
4. A letter from a national health care accrediting body putting the hospital on notice of decertification, based on severe deficiencies found on the last survey.
5. A follow-up letter from a major health insurance company indicating possible cancellation of approved provider status, as a result of the accreditation deficiencies.
6. A visit from the hospital's Chief of Surgery complaining bitterly about what he called the hospital's "abysmal housekeeping services."
7. A letter from a recently discharged patient inquiring about some missing jewelry and threatening a lawsuit.

Sister Mary Veronica rubbed her temples again. How would she sort all this out? There was just so much time in the day. Who should she respond to first? Where to begin? As she pondered those questions, she began to reflect on her recent teaching sabbatical.

LEARNING OBJECTIVES

- To identify further the concept of customers in the human services
- To describe customer categories
- To review special customer considerations

CUSTOMERS DEFINED

A review of Sister Veronica's week suggests a certain complexity in the question "Who is the customer?" First of all, in the health and human services arena, we are not used to using that term to describe the people we help. More common are terms such as *clients, residents, families, consumers,* and the like.

The literature on quality management uses the term *customer* to help organizations achieve a better focus. I define *customer* fairly broadly as "anyone who benefits from our work." This would surely include the clients, residents, and families we serve as the *primary* or *ultimate* customers of the organization but also extends to others who may benefit directly or indirectly from the organization.

In Sister Veronica's case, in addition to the patients and their families, the customers of her facility include the employees of this organization and the physicians and other health care providers affiliated with the Center. Sometimes referred to as *internal customers,* employees and other contract providers not only provide services to the primary customers but also benefit from the organization for their livelihood and professional identity. In addition, they rely on the work of one another in performing their work effectively.

A third category of customer is that of *stakeholders,* or people with special interests in the organization and who may benefit only indirectly from it. For St. Luke's, this includes the president of the local chamber of commerce, the national health care accreditation body, major funders such as the health insurance company, and others not listed here. Stakeholders may include funders of programs, accreditation or licensing agencies, advocacy groups, and the community at large. Although these groups are not the primary reason Sister Veronica's organization exists, they are criti- cal to its viability and survival and must be included in the development of performance criteria. These categories of customers, with representative samples from Sister Veronica's organization, are shown in Table 2.1.

This framework is meant to be a guide only and should not be viewed as rigid or prescriptive. It is not as important to get customer groups assigned to the "correct" categories as it is to be sure that all groups have been considered.

In the human services field, it is not at all uncommon to generate a long and varied list of customer groups. A few years ago, I did an informal survey of all 16 state agencies in the state of Missouri, asking representatives from each to identify their major customer groups. The result was amazing to me and is shown in Table 2.2.

Undoubtedly, one could add to the list. I was particularly interested in those agencies that identified "customer groups" that one would not ordinarily think of. For example, the Department of Natural Resources included trees, plants, and wild animals in its list of customer groups!

TABLE 2.1   Identification of Customer Categories for St. Luke's Community Hospital and Health Care Center

External Customers	Internal Customers	Stakeholders
Ultimate customers	Employees	Board of Trustees
Patients	Volunteers	Advisory boards
Families	Physicians and other	Accrediting bodies
	health care providers	Licensing agencies
Other		Insurance companies
Suppliers of goods		Unions
and services		Local community

SOURCE: Adapted from *Total Quality Management for Mental Health and Mental Retardation Services: A Paradigm for the '90s* (p. 38), G. V. Sluyter and A. K. Mukherjee, ©copyright 1993 by Gary V. Sluyter. Reprinted with permission of the first author and copyright holder.

The process of identifying the organization's customers and their requirements becomes the point of departure for other aspects of the organizational performance model, including the development of a vision, mission, and values. Typically, I begin with this issue as a first step when working with organizations on performance and strategic planning issues. (An expanded discussion will follow in Chapter 4.)

In the context of strategic planning, I ask employees of the organization to consider the following questions when working to identify their customers.

1. Who calls or comes to us for help?
2. What other groups of people depend on us or benefit (directly or indirectly) from our work?
3. Who else is interested in what we do?
4. Who would suffer a loss if we went out of business?

Through this kind of questioning process, we eventually fill in the blanks of the customer category grid illustrated in Table 2.1. As an added bonus, participants in the process begin to develop a broader and more balanced perspective of their organization and its work.

SPECIAL CUSTOMER CONSIDERATIONS

There are several special considerations regarding the customers of human services organizations. Unlike most of the customers of retail or service establishments (restaurants, hotels, department stores, etc.), who seek out those services willingly and voluntarily, sometimes the ultimate

TABLE 2.2   Identification of Major Customer Groups, All State Agencies in Missouri (1994)

Victims of crime	Environmental groups
Missouri cities	Teachers
Endangered species; the environment	Suppliers/vendors
Tourists	Banks, savings and loans
People with disabilities	Licensed professionals
Criminals and offenders	Hospitals
State employees	The media
Sportsmen	Service recipients
Schoolchildren/students	Employers
Agricultural commodity groups	Other state agencies
Farmers	Governor's commissions/committees
Citizens	Members of the legislature
Counties	Insurance companies
Law enforcement agencies	Regulated companies
The Environmental Protection Agency	

customers of human services organizations do not want help at all. For example, people do not usually look forward to being hospitalized, sent to prison, or forced by an employer to see a psychiatrist. In these cases, the distinction among customer groups may be very important to clarify.

For example, if Sister Veronica were to ask her ultimate customers what they want most from her organization, they might very likely ask to go home. If she were to discharge them before a clinically appropriate time, she may make those customers happy, only to run headlong into a wall of legitimate protest from other customer groups, especially health care providers, families, accreditation bodies, and so on (funders, on the other hand, may very well applaud her decision!).

The point here is that the wishes of the primary customer in the human service business are not always the final word in making decisions or in evaluating the organization's performance. Sometimes it is necessary to subordinate the interests of the ultimate customer to those of other stakeholders, such as funders. Within that structure, however, the human services organization can identify other important client outcomes to satisfy, such as desire to be treated with dignity and respect, to have accurate and timely information, and to be treated in a safe and healthy environment, free from abuse and injury.

Because of the unique nature of our business, we may sometimes find ourselves in situations in which there is conflict among our various customer and stakeholder groups. As state director of a mental health division, I often found myself in conflict with state legislators over client and employee issues. For example, our state department had a rigorous rule about client abuse. Whenever it was proven, we would terminate the employment of the guilty party.

Often, the employee would appeal to his or her state legislator, who would in turn reprimand us for being too tough on our employees. As a state senator once told me, "My daddy used to take the horse whip to me and it didn't do me any harm!" In this case, it was client versus employee in a win-lose situation with a stakeholder thrown in for good measure.

If we respond to the needs of the stakeholder over those of the client, the stakeholder win may become a losing proposition for our ultimate customer. The organization that pays little attention to the needs of either customers or stakeholders runs the risk of not surviving, and the one that ignores stakeholder requests in the expressed interests of the clients may suffer from a "funding source backlash" situation in which clients end up paying the price in the long run.

Although it does not always work, the best course is to try to follow Stephen Covey's advice to "seek win/win solutions" (Covey, 1990). In addition, the use of cross-functional performance teams is sometimes useful in finding solutions to difficult customer conflict situations and will be discussed in detail in Chapter 7.

Another special consideration relates to relationships between and among employees as internal customers of the organization. Too often, we find a kind of "silo" effect in organizations, with the various departments developing as isolated and independent entities that never really talk with one another. This leads to conflict, turfism, and a loss of organizational productivity.

By helping employees view themselves as internal customers who are active partners in critical customer-supplier chains, the organization can begin to break down these barriers. For example, at St. Luke's, the maintenance department had long-standing conflicts with nursing staff. Anytime something broke down on one of the wards, there was a great deal of mutual finger-pointing. Maintenance would blame the nurses for negligence, and the nurses would blame maintenance for being lazy, unresponsive, and incompetent.

Sister Veronica intervened by helping both sides recognize the interdependence of their relationships. Nursing depended on maintenance for technical assistance and timely service, and maintenance depended on the nurses for timely notification, cooperation, and some basic preventive maintenance. This clarified the nature of the two-way customer-supplier relationships that existed between the departments.

Through a series of negotiations, both sides identified the outcomes that they would help each other achieve and signed a mutual agreement or interdepartment contract clarifying those outcomes, along with strategies for resolving problems. One feature of this new relationship was an agreement that the nurses would take care of certain "routine" maintenance items, once the maintenance staff had supplied them with a set of tools and basic instruction on their use. This left the maintenance staff free to concentrate on the more exotic and unusual problems.[1]

The thing I like the most about this understanding of the customer-supplier relationship is the mutual interdependence required to make it work. When organizations understand and apply these ideas, they begin to break down the silos that separate the various departments and units and strive to find ways of satisfying their various "internal customers."

Finally, you may wonder why I placed *suppliers of goods and services* within the External Customer (Other) category. Even though St. Luke's is itself the primary customer of its various suppliers (materials, supplies, food, etc.) I include suppliers in the customer category to emphasize the point made above about the dual nature of customer-supplier relationships.

As a customer, the hospital wants high-quality services and goods from its suppliers, but to get those things it must provide suppliers with signed contracts, accurate specifications, timely orders, proper payments, and so on. In effect, St. Luke's is both supplier and customer to the various vendors on which it relies. This is another expression of the interdependent nature of customer-supplier relationships and important to a complete view of organizational performance. Another way to view suppliers is as partners in the process of developing and delivering services.

Now that we have looked at some ways of sorting out various customer groups, let us examine how to determine customer requirements, that is, what our various customers want and need from us and how we respond to those requirements.

CHAPTER NOTE

1. This scenario is based on an actual example from a comprehensive mental health center in Charleston, West Virginia (personal communication with John E. Barnette, Chief Executive Officer, 1996).

REFERENCES

Covey, S. (1990). *The seven habits of highly effective people: Restoring the character ethic.* New York: Simon & Schuster.

Sluyter, G. V., & Mukherjee, A. K. (1993). *Total Quality Management for mental health and mental retardation services: A paradigm for the '90s.* Annandale, VA: American Network of Community Options and Resources.

IDENTIFYING CUSTOMER REQUIREMENTS

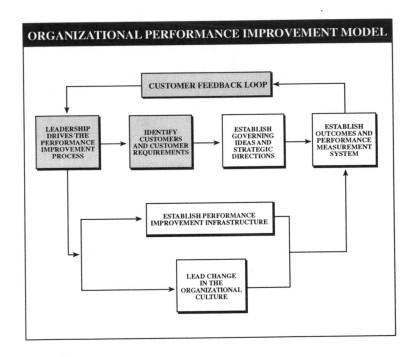

CHAPTER 3
IDENTIFYING CUSTOMER REQUIREMENTS

TWIN OAKS EXTENDED CARE FACILITY

Mary Maloney was frustrated! As administrator of the Twin Oaks Extended Care Facility, she was used to dealing with problems, but right now, she was feeling a little overwhelmed.

Last week, there had been two as-yet-unexplained resident deaths, followed by an outbreak of shigella on Ward B. Then she had three of her best LPNs resign because of their dissatisfaction with working conditions. Family members seemed overly demanding, she noticed a smell of urine again on Ward C, and the Joint Commission on Accreditation of Healthcare Organizations was scheduled for a site visit next week.

It was just after 6:00 p.m. when Mary finally had a chance to sit down and look over her mail. It was the usual stack of stuff: advertisements, department reports, letters of complaint, phone calls to return, and so on. One item caught her eye, a letter from a local consulting firm offering to conduct surveys of the facility's employees, clients, and clients' families. The purpose, it seemed, was to give organizations some data about customer expectations.

Mary smiled inwardly. It seemed to her that she didn't need some outsider to come in and tell her what people needed. She had worked in this field for more than 20 years and surely knew by now what was best for them. She tossed the letter into the trash and picked up one of her nursing journals.

She was just about to turn off her light and leave for the night when she got an emergency call. One of the residents had just fallen on a slippery floor and apparently broken her hip. With a deep sigh, she closed her office door and hurried toward the wards.

LEARNING OBJECTIVES

- To introduce the concept of "customer requirements"
- To discuss technical and perceptual aspects of quality
- To identify the special nature of quality in human services
- To discuss the notion of dimensions of quality
- To introduce the use of customer report cards

In Chapter 1, we defined organizational performance as "the organization's overall effectiveness in meeting the identified needs of each of its constituent groups through systematic efforts that continuously improve its ability to effectively address those needs." Given that definition, in order to understand organizational performance, we must first understand the nature of what our customers need and want from us, then somehow quantify and track our efforts to meet those demands. Like Mary, we may *think* we know what our various customers want from us but not really understand those needs at all.

TABLE 3.1   What Do Our Customers Want? Self-Advocates Speak Out

---

1. We are people and don't want to be labeled.
2. Focus on our abilities, not on our disabilities—what we *can* do, not what we *can't*.
3 Accept us as we are, not as you wish we would be.
4. We don't want to be abused, ridiculed, or shoved aside.
5. We *do* want your love and *support* (this is *very* important).
6. We want respect and understanding—see *our* point of view.
7. *Listen* to us. Don't tell us what to do . . . *ask* us what we want.
8. We want to feel good about ourselves and to have our rights respected.
9. Raise your expectations—we can do more than you think.
10. Allow us to make mistakes.

I worked for many years in the field of mental retardation and have maintained membership in the American Association on Mental Retardation (AAMR), the premier professional organization in the field, more than 100 years old. Once a year, the association holds a national conference that includes a rich variety of presentations on various aspects of services to people with disabilities.

One year, I was pleased to see that the association had included a session for various groups of "self-advocates," primary consumers who had begun to organize themselves for mutual benefit. I attended their session and was intrigued by their perspective on the services that they had received from us "professionals" over the years. At one point, I stood and asked them to tell us what they wanted or needed from us. They were not bashful at all and gave me a list of 10 things they wanted the most. These are listed in Table 3.1. As odd as it may sound, I can't remember anywhere in all my training, academic preparation, or experience that I was taught to view my work from the client's perspective, yet to assume we know what clients want from us may very well lead us down the wrong trail.

The notion that organizational performance must be evaluated from the perspective of the customer is central to the teachings of quality management. Martin (1993) provides a very helpful review of this idea as applied to human services, emphasizing the view that quality is "defined by the customer." When I heard Deming say that at one of his 4-day seminars in 1991, I was admittedly both intrigued and disturbed by the idea that our customers were the final arbiters of our performance. What about the role, for example, of "professional standards" and the results of years of research? Do these things we learn to hold so dear count for nothing?

As Martin (1993) has observed, the idea that our customers define what is meant by "good service" runs somewhat contrary to a long tradition in the human services field concerning the role of the "professional" in defining what is good for the client. In many cases, people come to us for help precisely because they do not have the ability, resources, or mental clarity to make decisions for themselves. To reconcile these views, we must, as Martin suggests, "make some pragmatic adjustments" (Martin, 1993, p. 34).

The way in which I reconcile these views is to recognize two issues in defining organizational performance or service quality. The first has to do with external standards, professional judgment, best clinical practice, and so forth. This is the *intrinsic* or *technical* dimension. The technical dimension evolves over time, through such things as professional disagreements, new data, compromise, trial and error, and scientific breakthroughs.

For example, when I began working in the human services field in the 1960s, the "treatment of choice" for people with mental retardation was the public institution. The push for "community alternatives" such as group homes and independent living arrangements was just beginning to emerge. Now, the new service paradigm has all but replaced the public institution as the treatment of choice for people with disabilities.

The second issue in performance or quality has to do with customer or constituent *perception*. Although this dimension may be softer and more prone to differences of opinion (different customers want different things), it is equally as important to consider in defining organizational performance.

When I worked as a superintendent of a public residential facility for persons with mental retardation, I had a parent (external customer) of a resident (ultimate customer) who would chastise me regularly for not arranging a 24-hour-a-day, one-to-one staff ratio for her daughter, who was confined to a wheelchair. Her definition of acceptable performance, in this case, was well beyond my perception of what the organization could reasonably provide.

In my opinion, and that of my professional staff, we were providing appropriate care for this young woman, well within acceptable clinical standards. Her mother, in our view, was expressing a multitude of anxieties through her overprotectiveness. We tried to help the mother deal with her guilt about her daughter's condition and to develop a more reasonable expectation of what we could (and should) do for her child, but in the final analysis, she was adamant in her demands for more intensive services.

Who was right in this case? If you take the position that quality is defined by the customer, then she was. If you believe, on the other hand, that quality depends only on meeting generally acceptable clinical standards, then we were. In reality, of course, we were both right and both wrong.

In the field of human services, we must consider both aspects of quality—the intrinsic or technical, and the role of perception—when evaluating our overall performance. To a great extent, our service recipients must rely on us to determine what is clinically appropriate for them. That's the "value added" dimension of our work. That's why we spend 6 to 12 years in the university learning how to provide good clinical services for people. That's why we hire people with specialized training and skills in a variety of service specialties to perform our work. That's why people who need help come to us in the first place.

On the other hand, we also need to pay close attention to what our service recipients and their representatives are telling us about their condition, their aspirations, and their needs. As observed by Martin (1993), the idea of listening to our clients and putting their needs first has long been a tradition in social and human service work. This is why I included item number 10 in the list of assumptions about quality management in Chapter 1; that is, the definition of quality rests on a skillful blending of input from both the customer and the provider.

For example, in mental health treatment, clients are involved in the development of their treatment plans through participation in an interdisciplinary team. When the process is working right, the final treatment plan represents a blending of professional opinion and client input. In a way, the traditions of our field have already given us a built-in "focus group" mechanism to help us hear the voice of the customer.

A complete view of organizational performance requires us to consider both the technical and the perceptual aspects of quality. Although there may be some overlap, these are fundamentally different. I have represented this view in Figure 3.1.

Quadrant I illustrates a situation in which organizations are paying a high degree of attention to technical or professional quality and a low degree of attention to customer concerns. For example, if Mary Maloney were to ignore the families who seemed to be overly demanding, she might only intensify her troubles when they took their complaints to the board of directors or the local newspapers. This is a "fire-fighting" position, in which the organization is constantly putting out fires or chasing complaints caused by a lack of attention to perceptual issues (good clinical services but poor bedside manner).

In a *Quadrant II* situation, the organization pays a low amount of attention on both technical and perceptual aspects of their performance. If Mary were to just shove the shigella problem under the rug, for example, she would be in grave danger of losing customers and/or feeling the wrath of her employees and stakeholders. She might even be at risk of going out

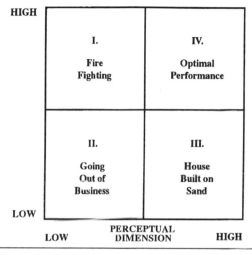

Figure 3.1. *Quality Dimension Grid*
SOURCE: The Quality Dimension Grid and parts of the discussion in the text are adapted from *Total Quality Management for Mental Health and Mental Retardation Services: A Paradigm for the '90s* (pp. 26-31), G. V. Sluyter and A. K. Mukherjee, ©copyright 1993 by Gary Sluyter. Reprinted with permission of the first author and copyright holder.

of business or, at the very least, being subjected to some unwelcome external pressures to change.

Quadrant III represents an organization that spends a great deal of time and attention on cosmetic or surface issues that placate the customer or stakeholder but do not deliver services of a good technical or clinical value. If Mary were to spend a great deal of time and attention creating a very pleasant and elaborate waiting room for families, for example, but hire unskilled nurses aides and not offer them adequate training, she would soon find herself in a very tenuous position with respect to technical or professional standards of practice. In effect, she would have built a house on sand that would eventually fall down around its very nice waiting room.

The ideal is to work toward *Quadrant IV,* in which the organization's leadership has defined its performance goals in terms of its ability to respond to both the technical and the perceptual dimensions of quality for all of its customer groups. In effect, to help an organization enjoy optimal performance, one must be able to respond to all the problems confronting it.

In summary, our human services organizations are in danger of committing two kinds of quality definition errors. On one hand, we can provide the best clinical services possible in a technical sense and still be rude and unresponsive to our customers. On the other hand, we can pay lavish attention to what the customer wants and still not achieve quality on the basis of clinical standards. What we need to do is strive for a good balance between the two elements of quality. The performance grid to be discussed later will attempt to strike this important balance.

THE SPECIAL NATURE OF
QUALITY IN THE SERVICE INDUSTRIES

Another adjustment we need to make when applying quality management philosophies to the provision of services has to do with the unique nature of the service delivery process itself. Quality management techniques grew out of a manufacturing environment and, as a result, must necessarily focus on the systems and processes for making a product, usually in an assembly line type of environment.

By the very nature of the work system, manufacturing organizations can establish quality standards for their products and make sure, through elaborate systems of inspection, that defects do not get to customers. Whereas Deming and others taught us that it is more expensive to throw defective products back than it is to change and improve the processes that created the defects, it is possible to improve quality in this way.

Not so in our business. Davidow and Uttal (1989) put it this way: "[Customer service] is intangible, so it eludes clear-cut measures of productivity. It's often produced, delivered, and consumed all at once, and by a human being, so it's hard to break down and control with any consistency" (p. 46).

When a company makes a toaster, it finishes the product, inspects it, packs it in a box, puts it on a truck, drives it across the country, loads it in a distribution warehouse, transfers it to another truck, and delivers it to the retailer, who in turn places it in the storeroom, marks a price, and places it on the display shelf. A customer buys the product, takes it home, and plugs it in. It may then blow up. In this case, a defective product made it through the inspection process and was delivered to the customer, who must now take it back to the store for a replacement or refund.

The point is that there is a very long time lag between the point that the product left the assembly line and when its quality was evaluated by the customer. Not so with human services, as noted above. Services are produced, delivered, received, consumed, *and evaluated* in a single instant of time. The implications of this reality are profound. It means essentially that we simply cannot manage quality in the human services in quite the same way we can in manufacturing. Once the service has been delivered, it is too late to take it back. Adding more inspectors or supervisors to maintain quality services just won't cut it. Instead, we need a different paradigm for how quality is produced in services and how we must manage and improve it.

One such paradigm for thinking about quality in human services is the concept known as the "moments of truth," introduced by Jan Carlzon (1987), president of Scandinavian Airlines System (SAS), to describe how service was delivered in his business. As defined by Albrecht (1992), a moment of truth is "any episode in which a customer comes into contact with any aspect of the organization and gets an impression of the quality of its service" (p. 26).

Any service encounter is made up of an entire cycle of moments of truth, from the beginning to the end of that unit of service. Albrecht (1992) refers to this complete sequence of moments of truth as the "cycle of service" (p. 118). It occurs every time one of our employees interacts with one of our customers or stakeholders. Furthermore, it establishes the basis on which our customers evaluate the overall performance of our organization.

Let me illustrate one cycle of service using a scenario from the Twin Oaks Facility.

You are the daughter of a resident of Twin Oaks. Your mother, now 86 years old, was admitted to the facility directly from the hospital after suffering from a severe stroke. She has lost many of her faculties and needs 24-hour-a-day skilled nursing care.

You come to the facility on a weekend for a visit. As you enter the parking lot, you cannot find a place to park. There are no allocated visitor spaces, and all the other spaces are taken. You wheel out onto a busy boulevard and park hazardously by the curb.

You approach the entrance to the building and notice that the outside light is broken and the door handle seems askew. In addition, the door is locked. You ring an unmarked buzzer and wait what seems to be a very long time.

Finally, the door is opened by a slovenly dressed person with a name tag that reads "Jim." You explain who you are and indicate that you want to visit with your mother. Jim sort of grunts, lets you in, and disappears.

Because this is your first visit to the facility, you are not sure where your mother's room is. You walk down a hallway and find what seems to be a nurses station. There are dozens of the facility's residents milling around the station. Some are using walkers, and others are in wheelchairs. All are only partially dressed. There is a distinct and unpleasant smell in the air.

You approach the nurses station and wait for the LPN in charge to look up from her charts. Finally, she glances your way, and you ask to see your mother. She yawns and begins to look up her name. She is interrupted by a phone call and pulls out another chart while apparently talking to a doctor. You wait patiently amid increasing noises from the residents near the nurses station.

Finally, the LPN gives you directions to your mother's room. You enter and find that she is sleeping. Her roommate is watching TV with the volume turned up. She ignores you, so you flag down one of the aides in the hall and ask her if she can help. The aide comes into the room, grabs the TV remote from the roommate's hand, and yells at her, "Mrs. Jones, I told you to keep the volume down! Are you stupid?!" With that, she turns the TV off, puts the remote in a closet, and leaves the room.

As a family member and customer of this facility, you have just experienced a sequence of moments of truth during your first visit. This cycle included a variety of impressions that the facility and its staff have made on you in a very short period of time, including parking problems, access to the facility, slovenly dressed and discourteous staff, distracted nursing staff, a chaotic environment, bad smells in the air, and an abusive aide.

Based on these moments of truth, you have formed an overall impression of this organization's performance, and it is not particularly favorable. Although you may give it the benefit of the doubt and check it out several more times before you move your mother to another facility, those impressions will stay with you. You may even tell others about your experience.

Research suggests that dissatisfied customers will tell between 10 and 20 other people about their bad experience with a service provider, whereas the satisfied group will share their good feelings with only a handful of others (Davidow & Uttal, 1989, p. 35). The effect on a service provider's organizational viability should be obvious. Even in the public sector, where the customer's evaluation may have a more indirect effect on organizational behavior, eventually negative evaluations influence the actions of stakeholders and those who control the purse strings (e.g., governors and legislators).

One way that the "moments of truth" idea can help you improve your organization's performance is to help your employees learn to "think like a customer" (Albrecht, 1992, p. 117). Create a scenario for your organization similar to the one above and use it in training sessions, asking your employees to place themselves in the customer role and evaluate the moments of truth.

The reality of how quality is managed in human service organizations, through sequences of moments of truth, brings us to the realization that all employees of the organization must have the philosophical frame of reference, training, and tools to manage quality themselves. This underlies the importance of determining dimensions of quality, to be discussed below, and of having very clear descriptions of the organization's governing ideas, which we will examine in Chapter 4.

DIMENSIONS OF QUALITY

In addition an understanding of "moments of truth," another important perspective with respect to defining performance in a service environment has to do with the dimensions of quality. In my seminars on Total Quality Management, prior to the lunch break, I ask participants to evaluate the restaurant where we eat lunch and bring back their perceptions of their experience. To help frame that exercise, I place a list of words on a flip chart: general environment (ambience), cleanliness, food quality, accessibility (e.g., parking), service quality, courtesy of staff, quantity of food, and variety of choices.

When we return from lunch, I return to the list and ask people to give the restaurant a score or grade relative to each word on the chart. I ask them to use a familiar grading system: A = *Excellent* to F = *Failure*. We generally have a spirited exchange during this process, as different people push for different grades on each item. (This process in itself demonstrates the perceptual dimension of quality and how complex the issue actually is.) We finally reach some kind of agreement on each item, and I list the grades. Then, I explain that not all the items or quality criteria carry the same weight. For example, having good food is important but not at all as important as having it roach free! We then argue about the relative

TABLE 3.2   Customer Report Card for Restaurant

Quality Characteristic	Weight	Grade	Score	Weighted (Weight × Score)	Total Possible (Points)
General environment	3	B	3	9	12
Food quality	5	B	3	15	20
Service quality	4	C	2	8	16
Quantity of food	4	A	4	16	16
Cleanliness	5	C	2	10	20
Accessibility	3	B	3	9	12
Courtesy of staff	4	C	2	8	16
Variety of choices	3	B	3	9	12
Totals				84	124 (67.7%)

SOURCE: Compiled from Albrecht, 1992.

weighting of each item, using a five-point scale (5 = *Very Important*; 1 = *Low Importance*). Finally, we convert the letter grades into numerical scores (A = 4, B = 3, C = 2, D = 1, and F = 0) and multiply each by the relative weight to get an overall score for each item, creating a customer report card (Albrecht, 1992) as illustrated in Table 3.2.

In this case, for these customers on this particular day, the restaurant scored an overall 84 out of a possible 124 points, giving it a 67.7% report card rating. Obviously, based on the perceptions of this customer group, the establishment would do well to make some improvements.

Once a baseline has been established, the managers of the restaurant can begin to track patterns and trends in the customer reports and focus their performance improvement efforts on those that are the most serious. In this case, the item of *cleanliness* has the largest discrepancy between actual and possible score and stands out as one of the first things to address.

If Mary were to apply this idea to the Twin Oaks Extended Care Facility, she would begin with an identification of the quality character-istics or attributes that her customers say are the most important to them. To obtain this information, Mary and her staff may have to use a variety of data collection techniques. Martin (1993) has identified seven such data collection approaches, including customer satisfaction surveys, focus groups, and test marketing (p. 35).

For a facility such as Mary's, I would most likely recommend a focus group or direct interview technique to obtain data on quality characteris-tics or attributes. The focus group is typically a group of five to seven customers who are invited to sit together with a facilitator or staff member to give their input on a given subject.

After describing the purpose of the focus group and answering any questions, the facilitator may ask a series of guided questions, such as, "What are some things that you like best about Twin Oaks? What did you do today that was the most enjoyable? What has happened to you lately that was unpleasant or that you didn't like? What do you think we could do here to make this a better place?" Notes should be recorded by the facilitator or a scribe for later analysis.

Because the data collected are mostly of a qualitative nature, a formal statistical analysis cannot be done. I favor the use of some type of affinity analysis in which the major ideas that emerge from the focus groups are first listed on separate index cards. The cards are then sorted into logical categories. Through that process, a picture begins to emerge that reflects quality attributes that are important to the organization's customers. The proposed list should then be reviewed by several customers or customer representatives for verification and to determine a weighting for the report card. The items chosen are then placed in a customer report card format and weighted, as shown in Table 3.2.

Sometimes I use a focus group to develop a set of questions that might be used on a questionnaire, and other times I use the focus group to go deeper into data collected from questionnaires themselves. Whatever technique is used, it should be appropriate to the communication level of the customers and should respect the confidentiality of their individual responses. Also, each participant should receive a follow-up letter of thanks with some general information about the results.

Once verified with the customers of the facility, this report card can be used to help evaluate several important aspects of the center's performance. For a comprehensive view, the Center may also take this approach with each of the organization's major customer groups, including families, employees, and stakeholders. The data collected will be important to the development of the organizational performance grid, to be discussed in Chapter 5.

Unfortunately, most organizations do not do a great job asking customers for feedback, nor are they very adept at using that information to improve performance. I once heard a human resources professional from a major airline discuss his company's approach to obtaining customer satisfaction data. He described a very elaborate process that included the use of surveys, focus groups, benchmarking, and the like. When asked what the company did with all that information, he responded (with a straight face, mind you) that it analyzes the data, prints it out, and files it in the human resources office!

Unfortunately, I often get similar responses from people in human services organizations when I ask about how they use consumer data. Typically, they tell me that they collect it to satisfy some accreditation or licensing agency and then put it away in a file cabinet.

The real trick to identifying important quality characteristics is to place oneself in the shoes of the customer. As service providers, we tend to see things from a fairly narrow point of view and do not always appreciate the perspective of the person on the other side of the desk. Unless we have some procedure in place to ask our customers about their expectations and requirements, we will not obtain a clear and accurate picture and may build our service structure on a distorted notion of those needs.

Research by Zeithaml, Parasuraman, and Berry (1990) on the issue of quality dimensions in the service sector suggested five major quality factors that were most often identified by customers: *reliability, responsiveness, assurance, empathy*, and *tangibles*, with *reliability* ranking as one of the most important. As customers of service organizations, we have certain expectations about the performance of those organizations, even though they may not be stated explicitly. Furthermore, if we go to a service provider and receive good service, we expect the same on our next visit and are quite disappointed if it is not provided.

I had a recent experience with a hospital that brought the notion of multiple customers and their varying expectations home to me. My mother had been admitted to the hospital for a fairly serious stroke. I had to travel a great distance to be with her, as did several of my sisters. When we arrived, we met at the hospital and immediately tried to get some information about our mother's condition. For several days, we experienced the "nursing shuffle" as one shift after another supposedly passed our request on to the next shift, to the attending physician, to the specialist, and so on. It took a long time before we finally tracked down someone who would sit down and answer our questions.

My evaluation of that situation is that this hospital simply did not include family members in their list of "customers." Accordingly, it had made no efforts to assess what family members needed from the hospital, nor made any efforts to provide those things. I sat down and made a list of the quality attributes I wanted as a family member and listed them in customer report card format, as shown in Table 3.3. (I also gave a grade to the hospital in question.)

In my view, this hospital was paying attention to only some of the important quality attributes for family members and was failing miserably

TABLE 3.3   Customer Report Card for Family Members of Hospitalized Patients

Quality Characteristic	Weight	Grade	Score	Weighted (Weight × Score)	Total Possible (Points)
Access to medical staff	5	D	1	5	20
Responsiveness of nursing staff	5	F	0	0	20
Staff expression of concern	4	F	0	0	16
Information on patient's condition	5	D	1	5	20
Comfortable place to wait	5	C	2	10	20
Availability of close parking	5	B	3	15	20
Access to telephones	4	C	2	8	16
Access to cafeteria	4	A	4	16	16
Restroom availability	5	A	4	20	20
Map of hospital	4	C	2	8	16
Totals				87 (47.3%)	184 (100%)

on the rest. A hospital may be accredited by the Joint Commission on Accreditation of Healthcare Organizations and still not respond to the needs of all of its constituent groups.

In Chapter 5, we will examine how an organization uses these quality characteristics to develop an overall performance monitoring tool. First, let us consider the vital role of leadership in setting a clear direction for the organization and in shaping its culture for high performance.

REFERENCES

Albrecht, K. (1992). *At America's service: How your company can join the customer service revolution*. New York: Warner Books.

Albrecht, K., & Bradford, L. J. (1990). *The service advantage: How to identify and fulfill customer needs*. Homewood, IL: Dow Jones-Irwin.

Carlzon, J. (1987). *Moments of truth*. New York: Harper & Row.

Davidow, W. H., & Uttal, B. (1989). *Total customer service: The ultimate weapon*. New York: Harper Perennial.

Martin, L. L. (1993). *Total Quality Management in human service organizations*. Newbury Park, CA: Sage.

Sluyter, G. V., & Mukherjee, A. K. (1993). *Total Quality Management for mental health and mental retardation services: A paradigm for the '90s*. Annandale, VA: American Network of Community Options and Resources.

Zeithaml, V. A., Parasuraman, A., & Berry, L. (1990). *Delivering quality service: Balancing customer perceptions and expectations*. New York: Free Press.

Chapter 4

CHARTING A COURSE
FOR THE ORGANIZATION
The Vital Role of Leadership

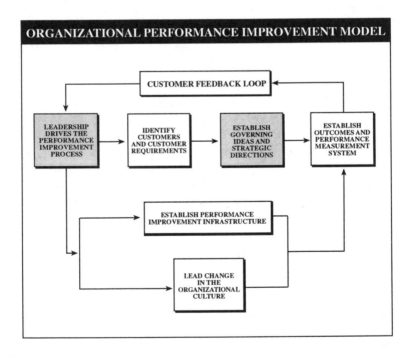

ORGANIZATIONAL PERFORMANCE IMPROVEMENT MODEL

CUSTOMER FEEDBACK LOOP

LEADERSHIP DRIVES THE PERFORMANCE IMPROVEMENT PROCESS

IDENTIFY CUSTOMERS AND CUSTOMER REQUIREMENTS

ESTABLISH GOVERNING IDEAS AND STRATEGIC DIRECTIONS

ESTABLISH OUTCOMES AND PERFORMANCE MEASUREMENT SYSTEM

ESTABLISH PERFORMANCE IMPROVEMENT INFRASTRUCTURE

LEAD CHANGE IN THE ORGANIZATIONAL CULTURE

CHAPTER 4
CHARTING A COURSE:
THE VITAL ROLE OF LEADERSHIP

NOTE: Materials from Fulton State Hospital, Gateways, Inc., New Hope Village, and Shawnee Hills, Inc. and used by permission.

NORTHWEST REHABILITATION CENTER

Dave Schmidt was getting ready to address his employees in a general staff meeting. Ever since taking over as Executive Director of the Northwest Rehabilitation Center about a year ago, he had been encouraged by the dedication of his staff. Northwest was a private, not-for-profit rehabilitation facility for adults with mental and physical disabilities in the Capitol City area, and Dave felt that it was one of the best in the state.

Still, in spite of his assessment of the multitude of services and programs offered by the Center, he had a vague feeling that something was missing. There seemed to be a lack of focus, an unclear vision about the direction in which the Center was heading. Since taking over as director, Dave had been content to maintain things as his predecessor had set them up, and things seemed to be going well. Lately, though, he had a growing feeling that this apparent success might be creating a level of complacency that might not be productive.

Looking through some reference material for his speech, Dave noted something he had previously overlooked. It was a little card on which was printed the following:

Northwest Rehabilitation Center
"Because We Care"

Statement of Mission

It is the mission of the Northwest Rehabilitation Center to provide the highest possible quality rehabilitation, treatment, and other appropriate clinical services to adults with mental illness, developmental or physical disabilities, or related conditions, to help those people achieve their maximum potential as fully functioning citizens of Capitol City. To this end, we pledge to provide our services in the least restrictive environment possible according to each person's individualized rehabilitation plan, to always treat our clients with dignity and respect, and to provide services without consideration of one's ability to pay.

Reflecting on the words, Dave had two reactions. First, the statement seemed a bit wordy. He wondered if his staff really understood it. Second, what was the process for developing and revising it? He made a note to ask his staff those questions at the staff meeting.

LEARNING OBJECTIVES

- To discuss leadership's vital role in organizational performance
- To examine the process of developing organizational governing ideas
- To introduce a strategic planning model and demonstrate how governing ideas are integrated into the planning process

ORGANIZATIONAL GOVERNING IDEAS

Dave's questions about his organization's mission statement were timely and on target. Many organizations have spent a great deal of time and money developing statements like the one above, finally displaying them prominently in expensive frames, only to find that they do little more than adorn the corporate hallways. The establishment of a clear mission for the organization is vital to improving performance, but that mission must be one that is understood and lived on a daily basis by all employees.

Clarifying the organization's governing ideas (Senge, 1990) is a special responsibility and privilege of leadership. Even if the day-to-day affairs of the organization are managed well, without a shared understanding of the mission, vision, and values, the organization embarks on a rudderless course toward an unknown destination. The end result is a great deal of wasted human and material resources, along with a lackluster performance record.

Bennis and Nanus (1985) make an important distinction between leadership and management by suggesting that, "Managers are people who do things right. . . . Leaders are people who do the right things" (p. 21)

Leaders set direction and vision for the enterprise; managers do what is needed to keep it on that course. High-performance organizations need people with both skills. Sometimes both talents are found in the same person; sometimes they are not. The important thing is that whoever is in charge recognizes the importance of both elements and sees that they are in place. The process itself can be an exciting and involving effort.

I have found Senge's (1990) conceptualization of mission, vision, and values as the organization's "governing ideas" to be particularly helpful. These terms are sometimes used interchangeably in the literature, and I am grateful to Senge for his clarification of the differences.

Mission: The organization's purpose for being, its identity

Vision: The organization's picture of what it wants to become, its destiny

Values: The philosophy or set of core principles that helps guide the organization in accomplishing its mission and realizing its vision

---

Adopted 1/1/96

MENTAL HEALTH LEADERSHIP TRAINING PROGRAM

A university-based leadership development program for mental health professionals

MISSION

Our mission is to help our customers develop the leadership and managerial skills needed to support the effective delivery and continuous improvement of mental health services.

VISION

To earn a national reputation as a valued resource for training in applied leadership and management for mental health professionals.

VALUES

In support of our mission and vision, we pledge to develop and offer training services that

- are of the highest quality and relevance to our customers' needs;
- help improve our customers' leadership and managerial effectiveness;
- are cost-effective and perceived by our customers as a good value;
- are being continuously improved on the basis of new ideas and customer feedback;
- are always delivered with integrity, professionalism, and respect.

Any organization, large or small, can benefit from taking some time to evaluate its purpose, direction, and philosophical premises. Stephen Covey (1990) counsels us to do the same for our own personal lives. Even though my leadership training program has a staff of only one (me), I feel that it is vital to have a set of governing ideas for my work.

Let me point out a couple of things about this set of governing ideas. First, they are not static (note that they are dated). I first developed them about 5 years ago, and the first draft looked considerably different from the latest rendition. I work with these statements, continually seeking to simplify the language and increase the understandability and usefulness. For me they are dynamic.

Also, I have found that they help keep me on track and on target. Often, I have certain opportunities that look attractive in terms of money or recognition. I always try to evaluate them against my governing ideas to determine consistency. If the new opportunities seem too far afield, I may very well pass on them. This is important in maintaining a clear focus and constant direction.

Here are a few guidelines to help organizations with the development of a set of governing ideas. First of all, ask these questions when thinking about each one.

MISSION

1. Who are our customers or beneficiaries?
2. What do they want/need from us?
3. What are our major products or services?
4. Why do we exist?
5. What do we do best?
6. What customer outcomes are the most important?
7. How do we measure success?

VISION

1. Where are we going as an organization? What do we want to become?
2. What are the most important key issues that we must address in order to successfully carry out our mission and help shape our destiny?
3. If we had a magic wand and could transform our organization into anything we wanted, what would it look like?
4. If we won an award for being the most excellent organization of its kind in the world, why would we have received it?
5. If we got an unrestricted foundation grant for $5,000,000 to improve our organization, how would we spend it?
6. How do we want to be viewed by our various customers and the public?
7. If we climbed into a time machine, went 15 years into the future, and stepped out into our organization, what would it look like?

VALUES .

1. What are our most important principles or beliefs?
2. What are some of the most deeply held traditions of our organization?
3. What is our reputation in the community or among our professional colleagues?
4. What is an example of how we stuck with our basic values though it was not profitable?
5. What is an example of how we abandoned our basic values to obtain short-term gains?

6. What are some principles or guidelines that we do not follow but that we might want to consider adopting?
7. How do our customers think we should behave?

In addition to these questions, I suggest several general guidelines.

1. Governing ideas are developed by the leaders of the organization, with input and review by representatives from all customer groups and stakeholders.
2. Revisit and revise mission, vision, and values statements (if necessary) periodically—at least annually.
3. Go for simple, clear, and straightforward language. Avoid jargon, alphabet soup, and "bureaucratese."

In the example at the beginning of the chapter, Dave was correct in showing some concern about the wordiness of the mission statement. A shorter, simpler, and clearer version of that statement might read more like this:

NORTHWEST REHABILITATION CENTER

A private, not-for-profit, community-based rehabilitation center for adults with mental and physical disabilities

The mission of the Northwest Rehabilitation Center is to help people increase their capabilities to live and work independently in the community.

We do this by providing high-quality treatment and rehabilitation services that meet each individual's needs in a caring environment.

This statement communicates more to me than the other one. It avoids some of the jargon ("least restrictive environment," "maximum potential as fully functioning adults") and lays out clearly the Center's purpose and ultimate customers.

A fourth general guideline is to apply three tests: the "Mother Test," the "Last-Person-Hired Test," and the "Hair-on-the-Back-of-Your-Neck Test." When groups have developed their draft statements, I like to have them evaluate them using these three tests as follows.

Mother Test: If you called your mother (or someone's mother) and read her your statement, would she understand it? If not, you might want to continue simplifying the language.

Last-Person-Hired Test: Find the last person hired by your organization and, after this person has received basic orientation to the organization and the mission statement, ask him or her what it means in the new job. If the person cannot answer the question easily, take a look at the statement for clarity of meaning.

Hair-on-the-Back-of-Your-Neck Test: When you read the statement, do you get a little tingle at the back of your neck? If not, the statement may not have enough power to drive people's behavior. It should generate some excitement, some enthusiasm for the work.

A fifth guideline is that format is not important, but understandability is critical. It doesn't matter much how the statements are packaged, as long as they are clearly understood by all customer groups, including employees and stakeholders.

When I work with organizations on the development of missions and other governing ideas, I generally do it in the context of a 1- or 2-day planning retreat with 25 to 30 staff members drawn from several levels of the organization. In addition, I suggest that some customers be present, as well as representatives of key stakeholder groups. Sometimes this includes clients or family members and members of the board of directors or funding agencies. Through the retreat process, we develop draft statements of mission, vision, and values for later verification by customer and stakeholder groups.

One organization I worked with on the development of governing ideas was the Fulton State Hospital in Missouri. Fulton developed a novel approach that it found useful. After the planning retreat, the superintendent asked the 30 participants to form teams of 2 or 3 people each and asked them to host meetings with small groups of employees to discuss the proposed statements and obtain their input. With almost 1,300 employees, this task took some time, but it proved well worth it.

At the end of the process, Fulton finalized the statements, then had them printed on parchment, framed, and hung on walls throughout the facility. In addition, the hospital had the statements printed on small cards and distributed to each employee. These statements are discussed in new employee orientation and other training sessions. A copy of Fulton's mission statement is included in the appendix to this chapter, along with those from a few other human service organizations.

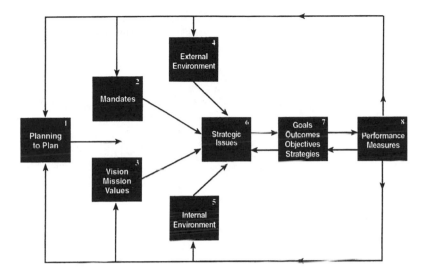

Figure 4.1. *The Strategic Planning Model*
SOURCE: Adapted from *Missouri Integrated Strategic Planning: Model and Guidelines* (Figure 4, p. 15), Office of the Governor of Missouri, ©copyright 1996 by Office of the Governor of Missouri. Reprinted with permission.

As I mentioned before, the development of governing ideas is only part of the process. It is important that the organization follow through by making sure that all employees understand what these ideas mean to them in reference to their own specific work assignments. My experience is that this process is unending and must be monitored continuously to be sure that it is taking effect.

I also suggest to organizations that they consider the development of vision, mission, and values within the context of a strategic planning framework that includes other important components. I favor one that was developed by the Governor's Office in Missouri as part of an overall statewide planning effort. This model is displayed in Figure 4.1.

This conceptual framework helps place the organizational governing ideas into perspective as one part of an overall strategic plan. The governing ideas give shape, substance, and boundaries to the work to follow. For example, one stage in the planning process is the development of *key issues:* important barriers, problems, challenges, and opportunities that face the organization. Whatever key issues emerge, they should be con-

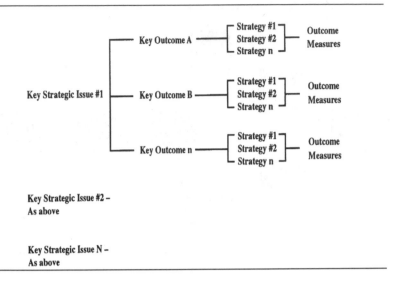

Figure 4.2. *The Strategic Planning Sequence*

sistent with the governing ideas. For example, if part of the agency's vision is to improve the quality of services for its ultimate customers, then one of its key issues might logically be "concerns about service quality."

I have modified the Missouri format slightly to help make it a little less cumbersome. Instead of all the components included in the interpretive guidelines for that model, I suggest an abbreviated sequence that includes only key strategic issues, key outcomes, strategies, and outcome measures, as shown in Figure 4.2. A complete example of one key issue for the Northwest Rehabilitation Center is shown in Box 4.1.

Once the organization has clarified its basic governing ideas and identified other aspects of its strategic plan, it is ready to proceed with a set of criteria that will be used as a framework for measuring performance. This concept will be developed further in Chapter 6. Before we leave the discussion of leadership's role in organizational performance, however, we need to take a look at the impact of organizational culture on performance.

BOX 4.1. *Northwest Rehabilitation Center Strategic Plan*

Key Strategic Issue #1: Employees of Northwest Rehabilitation Center (NWRC) do not have knowledge and skills necessary to consistently meet the needs of clients, families, and the community.

Key Outcome #1: NWRC will have a staff education program that helps employees continuously develop the knowledge and skills needed to consistently meet the needs of clients, families, and the community.

Strategies

1. NWRC will establish a staff development improvement team that will provide guidance and oversight for the agency's staff education program. The team will be made up of a cross section of employees from both the clinical and support sides of the house and will be established by September 1, 19xx.

2. The staff development team will conduct an analysis of training needs of all agency employees and provide a report to the Staff Development Team by January 15, 19xx.

3. Based on the results of the survey and analysis, the staff development team will propose a comprehensive, competency-based core curriculum for all agency employees by June 30, 19xx.

4. The staff development unit of the agency will pilot test the competency-based curriculum between July 1 and August 31, 19xx, and will propose revisions for implementation on October 1, 19xx.

5. Agency employees will complete the required core curriculum by July 31 of the following year.

Outcome Measures

1. Milestones in the development of the core curriculum
2. Number of employees completing the required training
3. Skill test scores of employees completing curriculum
4. Improved performance of employees on job tasks as measured by supervisors or assessments
5. Evaluations of the curriculum by participants
6. Percentage of compliance with external accreditation standards regarding staff training requirements

APPENDIX

ORGANIZATIONAL MISSION STATEMENTS

This appendix includes sample mission statements from several behavioral health care organizations. These organizational mission statements are used with the permission of the respective agencies.

Fulton State Hospital
Fulton, Missouri

We help people with serious mental illness and behavioral problems develop the skills for a more independent and meaningful life through quality assessment, treatment, and rehabilitation.

Gateway Center for Human Services
Ketchikan, Alaska

As a community resource, we join with people as they discover and achieve their paths to a healthy, satisfying life.

New Hope Village
Carroll, Iowa

The mission of New Hope Village is to enrich the quality of life for individuals with disabilities by offering opportunity, choice, and support in an environment which promotes dignity and self-fulfillment.

Shawnee Hills, Inc.
Charleston, West Virginia

To exceed your expectations

Gateways, Inc.
St. Louis, Missouri

. . . in partnership with people who have disabilities

Mission

Gateways is in partnership to support people in being contributing individuals in their communities.

Vision

All partners are empowered to be active, productive members of their communities.

We celebrate diversity and encourage individuality in all aspects of life.

We accept the challenge of excellence by addressing the needs of the community.

We pursue financial stability through self-directed revenue and charitable support.

It is through our affiliation as a service unit of the National Benevolent Association of the Christian Church (Disciples of Christ) that we strive to achieve our vision.

Values

1. Service to our partners is our first and foremost priority.
2. We support each partner in reaching his or her highest individual potential.
3. We continuously improve our processes and services as each partner's needs change.
4. Each partner is encouraged to live in a safe and healthy environment, in the community of his or her choice.
5. We embrace the spirituality of our partners and treat everyone with respect.
6. We are committed to a team approach in all we do.

REFERENCES

Bennis, W., & Nanus, B. (1985). *Leaders: The strategies for taking charge*. New York: Harper & Row.

Covey, S. (1990). *The seven habits of highly effective people: Restoring the character ethic*. New York: Simon & Schuster.

Office of the Governor of Missouri. (1996). *Missouri integrated strategic planning: Model and guidelines*. Jefferson City, MO: Office of the Governor.

Senge, P. (1990). *The fifth discipline: The art and practice of the learning organization*. New York: Doubleday Currency.

Chapter 5

LEADING CHANGE IN THE ORGANIZATIONAL CULTURE

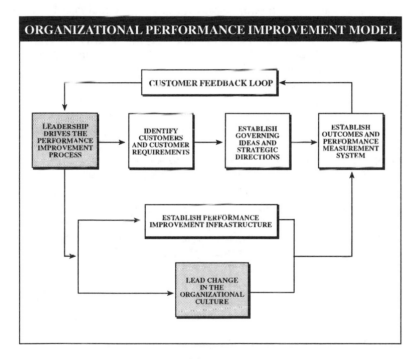

ORGANIZATIONAL PERFORMANCE IMPROVEMENT MODEL

CUSTOMER FEEDBACK LOOP

LEADERSHIP DRIVES THE PERFORMANCE IMPROVEMENT PROCESS

IDENTIFY CUSTOMERS AND CUSTOMER REQUIREMENTS

ESTABLISH GOVERNING IDEAS AND STRATEGIC DIRECTIONS

ESTABLISH OUTCOMES AND PERFORMANCE MEASUREMENT SYSTEM

ESTABLISH PERFORMANCE IMPROVEMENT INFRASTRUCTURE

LEAD CHANGE IN THE ORGANIZATIONAL CULTURE

CHAPTER 5
LEADING CHANGE IN THE ORGANIZATIONAL CULTURE

*MASON DETENTION CENTER
FOR JUVENILE JUSTICE*

It was a bright and clear spring day as George Moberly headed toward his office at the Mason Detention Center for Juvenile Justice in Metropolitan City. His mood, however, did not match the day. Since taking over as Chief Administrator a month ago, he had encountered one crisis after another, and he was feeling a growing concern about the Center's overall health. Mason had experienced a dozen administrators in as many years, and George couldn't help beginning to wonder about his own survival.

The Mason facility served about 120 adolescent boys and girls at any given time, plus another 75 or so in aftercare services. The buildings were in desperate need of repair, equipment and supplies were limited, and staff morale seemed very low. In spite of that, however, many of the employees had long tenure and were loyal to the facility.

It was that cadre of long-term employees that was a source of both comfort and anxiety for George: comfort because it was that core group that held things together in spite of a fairly high overall turnover rate, and anxiety because that group seemed to have its own ideas about how to do things and knew enough about the place to make sure that their way prevailed.

Even though George counted their expertise and experience among his assets, he was very concerned about some other aspects of that group. For example, he knew that they were the first to put down new ideas with such comments as, "We tried it that way once and it didn't work!" "Why bother, somebody else will come in and want it done differently," and "*They* just won't let us do that here!"

In his college courses, George had learned that he was dealing with something called the "organizational culture." He knew that the culture was a very strong influence in every organization and could help it move forward or cause it to stagnate. Furthermore, he realized that the culture was a tough nut to crack, being highly resistant to new ideas and slow to change.

As George turned into the detention center, he showed his ID badge to the guard, one of the "old-timers." As he drove through the gates, George thought he detected a slight smirk on the guard's face.

LEARNING OBJECTIVES

- To introduce the concept of organizational culture
- To discuss the phenomenon of "organizationally induced helplessness"
- To highlight the impact of organizational culture on performance
- To propose ways of leading organizational culture change

THE ORGANIZATIONAL CULTURE

George is quite accurate in his assessment about the challenges facing him when he tries to change the established organizational culture at Mason Detention Center. The fact that he has a group of long-term employees who derive certain benefits from the status quo will work strongly against him as he tries to lead change.

Many of the ideas we are discussing in this book are new to human service organizations and will likely create the same kinds of resistance in most organizations that George is feeling at Mason. Because the organizational culture is simply a reality with which we must deal, it is important to understand what it is and how its power can be enlisted in our performance improvement efforts.

Jablonski (1992) defines the corporate culture as "the set of values, beliefs, and behaviors that form its core identity" (p. 8). Elsewhere, I have suggested that the organizational culture includes at least eight dimensions: leadership style, agency governing ideas, communication patterns, approach to decision making, employee recognition, employee satisfaction, approaches to conflict resolution, and the basic approach to the management of quality or performance (Sluyter, 1995).

I have also characterized organizational culture as:

the nearly invisible but powerful force [that is] the glue that cements people and their behavior together in any organization, public or private. It is built up over time, may be at once both logical and illogical, may reflect overlapping layers of historical missions and visions, and can make or break any TQM effort. (Sluyter & Mukherjee, 1993)

Kotter and Heskett (1992) suggest that organizational culture can be viewed as having two levels, which differ in important ways. At one level (deeper, less visible, and more resistant to change), "culture refers to values that are shared by people in a group and that tend to persist over time" (p. 4). Organizational culture also exists at a more visible level as "the behavior patterns or style of an organization that new employees are automatically encouraged to follow by their fellow employees" (p. 4). Those behaviors may be more amenable to change than the shared group values.

Those authors also clarify the way in which organizational cultures develop. Citing the research of Schein and others, they suggest that the conditions that spawn organizational cultures are commonplace and develop through shared experiences over time that lead to success (Kotter & Heskett, 1992, p. 6). Furthermore, they offer the hopeful view that

TABLE 5.1   Typical Perceived Barriers to Quality in Mental Health Organizations

Quality of Services	Quality of Work Life
Bureaucracy	Personnel rules
Too much paperwork	Turf battles
Burdensome regulations	No input from staff
Rigid and restrictive processes	Too much control from the top
Inadequate staff training	Rumor mongering
Staff turnover	Stress levels
Limited financial resources	Lack of recognition
Conflicting policies	Low salaries
Poor communications	Lack of advancement
Unclear service mission	Lack of training
Staff burnout	Poor communication
Lack of customer focus	Lack of respect for staff

organizational cultures can be changed, given time, commitment, and the proper leadership (p. 12).

One of the things I am constantly confronted with when working with human services organizations is the powerful impact of culture on their *perceived* ability to improve. I often ask participants in my quality management seminars to list the barriers to applying TQM principles. A typical listing is shown in Table 5.1.

Although the existence of various barriers is not so surprising, what does intrigue me is the number of items that seem to reflect what Seligman (1990) refers to as "learned helplessness." Typical statements are the following.

"*They* won't let us do it."

"Management will kill the idea."

"We have tried this before and it didn't work."

"People here just aren't motivated to do much."

"The state personnel rules and regulations are too cumbersome."

"The unions will block it."

At first blush, it almost seems that people need some convenient excuses to justify not changing the way they do business. Even when I show them ways to deal with those barriers, there is a strong resistance to accepting those ideas. I think it is more than that, something that is caused by the very culture of the organizations in which we work. That's why I think Seligman's research is so relevant.

In the fall of 1964, Martin Seligman began his graduate studies at the University of Pennsylvania under the direction of learning theorist Richard L. Solomon (Seligman, 1990). While working in Solomon's laboratory, Seligman became interested in a series of experiments with dogs. The basic experimental design was to take a group of three dogs and test their reactions to mild shocks. One dog was given shocks from which it could easily escape, another was given shocks from which it could not escape, and the third dog (a control) was left alone.

Later, all three dogs were placed separately in one side of a shuttlebox, a two-chambered box divided by a low barrier. A shock was then administered to each dog, and their behaviors were observed by the experimenters. Consistently, the dog that had previously learned that he could escape from the shock quickly learned to jump over the barrier to safety. Likewise for the dog that had been left alone.

The other dog, however, the one that had previously learned through experience that nothing it did made any difference in lessening the shocks, simply lay down and did not try to jump over the barrier. Through dozens of experiments, Seligman developed the theory of "learned helplessness," applying it to people as well as to animals.

The gist of the theory is that when people are subjected over time to painful situations that they perceive as being out of their control, they may develop an expectation that nothing they can do will change things. Seligman believes that this notion of futility is at the heart of a national epidemic of depression (Seligman, 1990, p. 70). Fortunately, his research has also resulted in ways of countering this disturbing phenomenon, which he describes in his book *Learned Optimism* (Seligman, 1990).

McGrath (1994) reviewed some of the literature on this phenomenon in organizations, referring to it as "organizationally induced helplessness (OIH)." He cites the work of Agris, which suggests that:

There is an incongruency between the needs of an individual to become healthy and mature and the nature of bureaucracies, such as formalization, standardization, and rigid rules. Over time employees become shaped by the organization and are unable to demonstrate creative and mature behavior, even when it is desired and rewarded. (McGrath, 1994, p. 90)

McGrath (1994) identified several categories of factors that tend to induce the OIH phenomenon.

- Centralized or bureaucratic organizational structures,
- Rigid policies and procedures,

- A lack of perceived relationship between performance and appraisal and between performance and reward systems, and
- Leaders and supervisors blaming employees for problems and taking credit themselves for successes (pp. 90-91).

It is my observation that there is a great deal of organizationally induced helplessness in our human service organizations. I see it emerge when I work as a consultant to agencies interested in applying quality management to improving performance. Because of past experiences and strong conditioning, there are strong internal barriers to accepting the idea that employees of the organization can have any control at all over their own destiny or that of the organization. People seem so beaten down that they screen out any input that is contrary to this belief.

If learned helplessness is a part of the organization's culture, then it will be very difficult for employees to believe that they have any role in changing things. Like the dogs in Seligman's early experiments, they will just lie down, believing that they have no control over the shocks. On numerous occasions during my seminars on quality management that the expressions of cynicism and hostility have been so strong that I was forced to cease the lecture just to listen to employee concerns.

CHANGING THE ORGANIZATIONAL CULTURE

Changing the organizational culture is a difficult proposition, but it is up to leadership to begin the task. I suggest the following elements in a change model.

1. *Leadership Awareness:* Leadership recognizes that the existing organizational culture is out of sync with its performance improvement vision. As observed by the U.S. GAO report (1991), this is often characterized by a "history of excessive hierarchy, rigidity, and a relative lack of trust between labor and management" (p. 32). Leadership must accept the possibility that the current culture will not support the directions that it wants the organization to go and that it must work to change the culture itself. This awareness must carry with it both a commitment to do what is necessary and a compelling need to change.

Kotter (1996) suggests that establishing a sense of urgency is the first step in the organizational change process. It energizes people and helps move them away from organizationally induced helplessness, discussed above. It is up to leadership to generate that sense of urgency by identifying a compelling reason for change. That reason will vary from organization to organization and may include such things as competitive position within the service arena, demands of managed care, tight budgets, a lack of consumer and citizen confidence, client safety issues, or employee morale. Whatever the reason or reasons, they must be serious enough to help move people out of the comforts of complacency.

2. *Cultural Assessment:* Once leadership has accepted the fact that the culture must change and has begun broadcasting the rationale for the change, it begins to examine the existing culture to identify and understand the underlying values that shape it. One way to begin this process is to ask each member of the leadership team to complete the Organizational Culture Assessment Scale shown in Box 5.1. After that is completed and analyzed, the team can identify major cultural issues that need to be considered as part of the change process.

3. *Constructing a New Cultural Vision:* After the cultural assessment has been completed and discussed by team members, they can then begin constructing a vision of the culture they want to develop. One approach I use is an organizational development exercise in which I meet with the organization's key leaders (usually the Chief Executive Officer and those who report directly to this person) for the purpose of cultural visioning.

After discussing the idea of organizational culture and completing the assessment, I ask them to think about key characteristics of their current culture based on that review. Using a flip chart, I write down those ideas on the left side of the paper, dividing them from the right side with a vertical line down the center of the page.

When all the ideas are in, I then ask the group to think about aspects of an "ideal" culture, one that would fit most productively with the performance improvement model already outlined. If they had a magic wand, how would they like their culture to look? We then list those ideas down the right side of the page.

One such list, derived from a brainstorming session with the key executives of a large state agency, is shown in Table 5.2. Although there is no one organizational culture that is right for all organizations, there is some evidence that a more open and responsive culture is critical to high performance. The GAO report (1991) found that the executives in the successful firms included in the survey tended to define such a culture in terms of four attributes: "widespread information sharing; fewer formal and informal barriers between departments and among workers; a spirit of innovation; and a high level of employee satisfaction" (p. 32).

text continues on p. 59

BOX 5.1. *Organizational Culture Assessment Scale*

Below are listed brief descriptions of various organizational elements for two human service agencies. Both serve a similar client or customer population, and they have about the same level of funding and number of staff members. Both offer a wide array of similar services. Their organizational cultures (patterns of beliefs, values, and behaviors), however, are very different, as described below. After reading the descriptions for each of the organizational elements, rate your organization in the scales located at the end of the box.

Agency X	Agency Y
Mission, Vision, and Values No mission, vision, or value statements have been articulated; vague goals are stated; no description of primary customers or what they need; no training given on basic purpose or direction of the agency.	Clear mission, vision, and values statements have been developed with input from customers, employees, and stakeholders, based on customer identification and needs; all employees are trained on these concepts.
Leadership Style Major decisions are made by the executive committee and handed down the hierarchy; leadership style is "my way or the highway."	Executive committee makes broad policy consistent with the mission, vision, and values, and delegates the day-to-day operations; employee input is valued, encouraged, and rewarded.
Teamwork Infighting and intergroup warfare are the norms; strong tendency to "track the culprit and assign blame when things go wrong"; some committee work, but very little teamwork; no training or time provided for team efforts.	All employees work as a part of one or more performance improvement work groups or teams; within this framework, employees focus on quality problems and offer improvements; teamwork is rewarded, training is provided, and time is made vailable for team efforts.

BOX 5.1. *Continued*

Conflict Resolution

Conflict is suppressed by top management; the message is that everyone must get along and not "rock the boat"; any malcontents are quickly identified and their lives made miserable; people quickly learn to smile and "get even later."

Each employee is encouraged to deal with problems and conflict directly with coworkers, supervisors, and people supervised; specialized training is provided on positive conflict resolution techniques, and some staff are trained as team facilitators to help teams work through conflicts.

Quality

Quality is defined as compliance with external standards and internal rules; the quality assurance officer monitors adherence to standards and files "deficiency reports" when there are problems; no efforts to obtain input from clients or families about services provided.

Quality is only partly defined as meeting standards and rules; the Center's vision defines principles of quality, and each section works to apply them to its own area; the Performance Improvement Coordinator helps units both to learn to obtain data from all customer groups and to assess and improve heir performance.

Training

The staff development department provides basic orientation training for all new employees, and some training for others; many employees feel that training is not sufficient and that what is provided does not help them do their jobs better.

Each employee receives a very thorough orientation to the Center and follow-up training and coaching on his or her role in providing positive outcomes for customers; a formal system is in place to provide other training as needed and to recognize people for completing training.

BOX 5.1. *Continued*

Employee Recognition

Very few formal or informal employee recognition efforts exist within the agency; one employee remarked, "The only time we get recognized is when we screw up!"; the "Employee of the Month" program is seen as too political.

A formal and well-organized employee celebration system is in place; each unit routinely recognizes employees and teams for superior service; centerwide recognition programs are held quarterly.

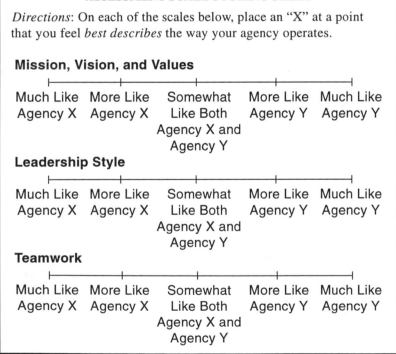

**ORGANIZATIONAL CULTURE
ASSESSMENT SCALE SCORING SHEET**

Directions: On each of the scales below, place an "X" at a point that you feel *best describes* the way your agency operates.

Mission, Vision, and Values

├─────────┼─────────┼─────────┼─────────┤

Much Like	More Like	Somewhat	More Like	Much Like
Agency X	Agency X	Like Both	Agency Y	Agency Y
		Agency X and		
		Agency Y		

Leadership Style

├─────────┼─────────┼─────────┼─────────┤

Much Like	More Like	Somewhat	More Like	Much Like
Agency X	Agency X	Like Both	Agency Y	Agency Y
		Agency X and		
		Agency Y		

Teamwork

├─────────┼─────────┼─────────┼─────────┤

Much Like	More Like	Somewhat	More Like	Much Like
Agency X	Agency X	Like Both	Agency Y	Agency Y
		Agency X and		
		Agency Y		

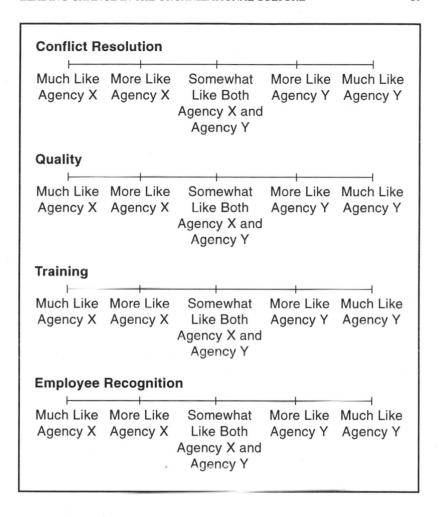

Conflict Resolution

Much Like Agency X	More Like Agency X	Somewhat Like Both Agency X and Agency Y	More Like Agency Y	Much Like Agency Y

Quality

Much Like Agency X	More Like Agency X	Somewhat Like Both Agency X and Agency Y	More Like Agency Y	Much Like Agency Y

Training

Much Like Agency X	More Like Agency X	Somewhat Like Both Agency X and Agency Y	More Like Agency Y	Much Like Agency Y

Employee Recognition

Much Like Agency X	More Like Agency X	Somewhat Like Both Agency X and Agency Y	More Like Agency Y	Much Like Agency Y

4. *Strategies for Cultural Change:* Once the leaders of the organization have developed a side-by-side profile like the one described above and have determined the key elements of their new cultural vision, they can then think about things they can do to move their organization from the left side to the right side of the page. Clearly, there are many things that are indeed out of their span of control. Laws, rules, and regulations from the legislature or the Governor's Office are difficult to change, and change may require time, negotiation, new proposals, and other efforts.

ANALYSIS AND DISPLAY OF DATA

When using this scale for multiple raters, anonymous individual ratings can be combined and displayed on a single scale, as shown in the example below.

Conflict Resolution

```
X
X
X        X
X        X
X        X        X        X
├────────┼────────┼────────┼────────┤
```
Much Like   More Like   Somewhat   More Like   Much Like
Agency X   Agency X   Like Both   Agency Y   Agency Y
                        Agency X and
                        Agency Y

In this example, the members of the group rating the organization had fairly similar views of their organization with respect to conflict resolution strategies. With some exceptions, there is a widely held perception that the organization tends to act much like Agency X. After the results of the ratings are displayed on a flip chart and discussed, members can begin exploring why perceptual differences exist. That discussion can lead to helpful insights into the organizational culture issues.

Many things are within their control, however. The employee recognition system is a good example. If the organization does not have a systematic approach to recognizing the contributions of employees, then one can be developed and pilot tested. Many of the issues on the left side of the page, in fact, can be given to teams of employees to work on, and the teams can then make recommendations to leadership. This is the team approach that we will examine in detail in Chapter 6.

5. *Periodically Assess Progress:* As the organization works to change the culture to be more consistent and supportive of performance improvement efforts, its leaders need to assess progress periodically. This can be

TABLE 5.2   XYZ State Agency Organizational Culture Assessment

Current Culture	Ideal Culture
Rule driven	Mission driven
Centralized decision making	Participatory decision making
Limited networking; insular	Team oriented
Lack of recognition and rewards	Meaningful reward/recognition system
"I'm not paid to think"	"I am responsible for ideas/suggestions"
Focused on inputs and activities	Focused on outcomes
Do things as always done	Try new things
Gossip mill communication systems	Open and accurate communications
Punishment driven (find culprit)	System improvement driven
Crisis driven	Controlled change
Rigid departmental silos	Few barriers among units

done informally by examining the vision from time to time to evaluate how well changes are being made. One way to do this is to ask the members of the leadership team periodically to complete the *Performance Improvement Progress and Cultural Change Scale* (Box 5.2).

One caution is offered regarding your expectations about detecting change in the organizational culture. It takes hard work and many years of concentrated effort to really turn an organization around. Masters (1996), discussing barriers to the success in implementing quality management, referred to Deming's contention that "it takes three to five years to fully implement TQM in an organization" (p. 53). The GAO report mentioned earlier (1991) cited one quality expert who estimated 6 years or more to induce such a change (p. 32).

It has been my experience that even with such timetables, organizations can begin to feel the benefits within a few years, particularly in terms of improved employee morale. Also, I have found that real progress begins to show when a "critical mass" of employees have begun to buy into the new model of organizational performance and the culture necessary to support it. I don't know exactly how to measure that critical mass, but I suspect that it includes virtually all the organization's leaders and about 30% of everyone else.

In the next chapter, we will begin examining the development of the performance improvement infrastructure, including a detailed examination of the use of performance improvement teams.

BOX 5.2. *Performance Improvement Progress and Cultural Change Scale*

Instructions: The purpose of this scale is to help you assess the impact of performance improvement strategies on your organization and its culture. On each of the organizational dimensions listed below, please rate the organization on any of the changes that you perceive may have occurred as a direct or indirect result of performance improvement principles and practices. Please use the following measurement scale:

−3	−2	−1	0	+1	+2	+3
Extremely	Negative	Slightly	No	Slightly	Positive	Extremely
Negative	Changes	Negative	Observable	Positive	Changes	Positive
Changes		Changes	Changes	Changes		Changes

1. *Organizational Values:* Changes in the way the stated values of the organization are reflected in the behaviors of staff, such as the degree to which staff interactions with customers reflect the values of the organization or unit.   −3 −2 −1 0 +1 +2 +3

2. *Organizational Structures:* Changes in the way in which the organization is structured to accomplish customer outcomes, such as a strict hierarchical/ bureaucratic structure versus the use of more flexible and decentralized teams.   −3 −2 −1 0 +1 +2 +3

3. *Leadership and Management Practices:* Changes in the way the formal leaders of the organization involve staff in decision making; the use of direct authority versus participative and empowering behaviors.   −3 −2 −1 0 +1 +2 +3

4. *Information:* Changes in the way data and information are used in the organization, such as the degree to which staff members receive feedback on important measures of organizational performance or customer outcomes   −3 −2 −1 0 +1 +2 +3

5. *Relationships:* Changes in the way staff members cooperate with each other, such as the degree of infighting versus mutual respect, cooperation, and teamwork.   −3 −2 −1 0 +1 +2 +3

6. *Competencies:* Changes in the way
staff members are encouraged/helped to
develop their skills, such as the degree to
which the organization is a flexible,
"learning" organization that values
employee training and development.   −3 −2 −1 0 +1 +2 +3

7. *Controls:* Changes in the manner in which
the organization manages staff behaviors,
such as close control and enforcement of
rules and regulations versus freedom to
innovate within broad boundaries.   −3 −2 −1 0 +1 +2 +3

8. *Rewards:* Changes in the way rewards
and recognition are managed by the
organization, such as the degree to which
formal structures and processes are in
place to recognize and reinforce positive
behaviors and performance.   −3 −2 −1 0 +1 +2 +3

9. *Innovation and Creativity:* Changes in the
way the organization supports innovation
and creativity, such as formal and informal
ways to encourage and reward new ideas. −3 −2 −1 0 +1 +2 +3

10. *Communication:* Changes in the way
communication flows in the organization,
such as multidirectional networks versus
strictly vertical and hierarchical lines.   −3 −2 −1 0 +1 +2 +3

Global Rating: On the whole, how do you
assess the changes occurring within the
organization as a result of the influence
of the cultural change and performance
improvement efforts in place?   −3 −2 −1 0 +1 +2 +3

Comments: It would be helpful if you would add any specific examples
of the positive or negative changes that you perceive for any of the
organizational dimensions listed above, as direct or indirect results of
cultural change and performance improvement efforts in place.

\# _____ _____

\# _____ _____

\# _____ _____

\# _____ _____

Thanks!

REFERENCES

Jablonski, J. R. (1992). *Implementing TQM: Competing in the nineties through Total Quality Management*. San Diego: Pfeiffer & Company.

Kotter, J. P. (1996). *Leading change*. Cambridge, MA: Harvard Business School Press.

Kotter, J. P., & Heskett, J. L. (1992). *Corporate culture and performance*. New York: Free Press.

Masters, R. J. (1996). Overcoming the barriers to TQM's success. *Quality Progress, 29*(5), 53-55.

McGrath, R. (1994). Organizationally induced helplessness: The antithesis of empowerment. *Quality Progress, 27*(4), 89-92.

Seligman, E. P. (1990). *Learned optimism*. New York: Knopf.

Sluyter, G. V. (1995). Total Quality Management and the organizational culture. *AMHA Leader, 15*(3), 1, 6.

Sluyter, G. V., & Mukherjee, A. K. (1993). *Total Quality Management for mental health and mental retardation services: A paradigm for the '90's*. Annandale, VA: American Network of Community Options and Resources.

U.S. General Accounting Office. (1991). *Management practices: U.S. companies improve performance through quality efforts* (GAO/NSIAD-91-190). Washington, DC: Author.

Chapter 6

MEASURING ORGANIZATIONAL PERFORMANCE

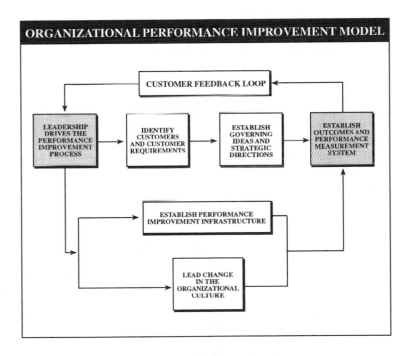

CHAPTER 6
MEASURING ORGANIZATIONAL PERFORMANCE

NORTH CENTRAL PSYCHIATRIC HOSPITAL

It was just after 6:00 p.m. when Carmen Torres finally had a chance to sit down and look over the latest data on her organization. As Superintendent of the North Central State Psychiatric Hospital, she wanted to stay current with available measures of performance. The problem was not that there was too little information—there was just *too much!*

Looking over the monthly printouts she received from the Department of Mental Health's central computer and the ones generated by her facility's management information system, Carmen was overwhelmed. Just last week, she had asked the Director of Quality Improvement to give her a report of all the types of data collected by the various sections of the organization.

The results were staggering and included every conceivable kind of statistic: pounds of laundry washed, meals served, income from Medicare, number of complaints from residents, incidents and injuries, medication errors, treatment plans completed, employee turnover, and so on. In fact, the Director of Quality Improvement counted more than 430 different measures of performance collected somewhere in the hospital.

The questions that haunted her were, "What kinds of data should we collect? Which of the measures are the most important? Which ones are relevant to overall organizational performance?" She was still wondering about those questions when there was a knock on her door. She opened it to find the Director of Quality Improvement with still another printout of 23 additional facilitywide performance measures.

———————

LEARNING OBJECTIVES

* To discuss approaches to the measurement of organizational performance
* To review methods for identifying organizational outcomes
* To introduce the use of an organizational performance grid

Carmen's questions go to the heart of how best to measure and monitor organizational performance. Too often, we have a great deal of data but not enough relevant information. The purpose of this chapter is to discuss a model for measuring and monitoring organizational performance based on a customer perspective.

Martin and Kettner (1996) discuss performance measurement in human services organizations, defining it as "the regular collection and reporting of information about the efficiency, quality, and effectiveness of human service programs" (p. 3). These three perspectives—*efficiency, quality,* and *effectiveness*—form the basis for the development of a com-

TABLE 6.1 A Performance Measurement Report for a Family Counseling Program

	Family Counseling Program		
	1999	2000	2001
I. Inputs			
A. Financial resources (in thousands)	$750	$800	$850
B. Human Resources (in FTEs)	22	24	26
II. Outputs			
A. Intermediate outputs (hours of counseling services)	27,500	30,000	32,000
B. Final outputs (service completions)	225	250	275
III. Quality			
A. Client satisfaction (percentage satisfied or very satisfied)	85	87	88
IV. Outcomes			
A. Intermediate (number of clients with no child abuse referrals)	112	125	150
V. Cost-Efficiency Ratios			
A. Cost per output	$27.27	$26.66	$26.56
B. Outputs per FTE	1,250	1,250	1,231
VI. Cost-Effectiveness Ratios			
A. Cost per outcome	$6,696	$6,400	$5,666
B. Outcomes per FTE	5.1	5.2	5.8

SOURCE: Reprinted from *Measuring the Performance of Human Service Programs*, L. L. Martin and P. M. Kettner, ©copyright 1996 by Sage Publications, Inc. Reprinted with permission.

prehensive performance measurement framework. An example is shown in Table 6.1.

This is a very helpful framework for identifying key measures of performance and can be used as one aspect of a measurement system based on the organization's customer and stakeholder groups. This system begins with a clear understanding of customer and stakeholder outcomes.

Martin and Kettner (1996) define *outcomes* as "the results, impacts, or accomplishments of human service programs as measured by quality-of-life changes in clients" (p. 51). Quality- of-life changes are those things that represent movement toward desirable client conditions or movement away from undesirable client conditions. Client conditions include "status, behaviors, functioning, attitudes, feelings, or perceptions" (p. 51).

For example, the primary customers of a city health department are the citizens of that community. Desirable conditions are such things as general health status, the use of health prevention measures, and longevity.

Undesirable client conditions might include such things as infant mortality, obesity, and heart disease. In addition, certain customer attitude factors may also be important in an overall evaluation of the department's effectiveness, such as satisfaction with the services. The key is to determine which outcomes are important to include in a measurement system.

DEVELOPMENT OF ORGANIZATIONAL OUTCOMES

Clarification of the organization's governing ideas is the beginning point of determining the major customer outcomes that are important for evaluating organizational performance. As we discussed in Chapter 3, this process begins with an understanding of our customers' requirements and expectations.

For example, leadership of the North Central State Psychiatric Hospital may discover the following outcomes as important to its various customer or stakeholder groups.

CLIENTS

- To be treated with dignity and respect
- To receive appropriate and timely services according to individual needs
- To get better as a result of the treatment or program
- To get out of the institution as soon as possible and maintain themselves successfully in the community
- To live in safe and healthy environments, free from harm and abuse
- To experience a decrease in psychiatric symptoms—to feel better

EMPLOYEES

- To be treated fairly by the organization
- To have good salary and benefits
- To have opportunities for growth
- To get good and timely information about what's going on in the organization
- To work in safe and healthy environments, free from injury and illness
- To have a secure job
- To be included in the organization's decision-making process

STAKEHOLDERS

- To have reliable and accurate information about fiscal and program matters
- To enjoy good stewardship of agency funds

- To see good outcomes for the organization's customers
- To enjoy a good reputation in the community
- To have a minimal number of adverse incidents and bad accounts in the press
- To have a voice in important decisions

Of course, customer outcomes will vary considerably on the basis of organizational type. As discussed in Chapter 3, some research will be needed to clarify and verify those that are the most relevant and valid for each organization. An accurate assessment of customer requirements and customer outcomes then forms the basis for the development of a framework for monitoring organizational performance. Sluyter and Martin (1996) discuss such a model for behavioral health care organizations. Based on a set of seven criteria, those authors proposed a sample performance monitoring grid for a public psychiatric hospital. They describe the model as follows.

> The structure of this grid is based on the identification of a family of measures that include the key constituent groups of the psychiatric hospital: Consumers, Employees, and Other Stakeholders. Within each constituent group are one or more *performance dimensions,* which describe the particular aspect of each constituent group being monitored; *statements of expected outcomes,* which are expressions of desired end-states for each area, based on the organization's strategic mission and plan; *performance measurement indicators,* which specify how the various outcomes will be measured; and *directionality* of desired trends. (p. 288)

This approach is based on the idea that successful organizations balance the concerns of all their key customer and stakeholder groups (Kotter & Heskett, 1992). As mentioned by Sluyter and Martin (1996), this is also known as a "family of measures" (Thor, 1995) or "stakeholder" (Daft, 1992) approach to organizational performance monitoring and is very consistent with TQM's emphasis on customers.

Accordingly, when constructing a performance monitoring system, organizational leaders must make sure that they are monitoring the outcomes that are the most important to each of the organization's customer or stakeholder groups. Because of this, the shape and content of each organization's performance monitoring framework will be unique.

For example, one community-based service organization for people with disabilities adopted a family-of-measures approach using a set of organizational outcomes called *"indicators of quality and stability,"* as shown in Table 6.2.

TABLE 6.2   Gateways' System of Outcome Measures: Indicators of Quality and Stability

Customer/Stakeholder Group	Indicators of Quality and Stability (Customer Outcomes)
Residents	1. All residents are free from abuse/neglect. 2. All residents live in safe and healthy environments. 3. Residents achieve outcomes stated in their personal plans. 4. All residents express satisfaction with their jobs and/or training programs. 5. 70% of residents have community supports.
Staff	6. Agency averages no more than 6 open positions, not to exceed 120 hours; positions are filled within 30 calendar days of closing. 7. Agency staff turnover is below 25% (projected annually). 8. All staff have current performance reviews. 9. Staff complete all required training within assigned timelines.
Fiscal	10. Agency's cashflow is positive. 11. Agency's expenditures do not exceed its revenues. 12. Gateways' average daily cost per resident for supported living is at or below the district, state, and national level.
Operational	13. Agency's problem-solving teams produce results, such as money savings, increased efficiency, or increased quality of services. 14. Stakeholders express satisfaction with quality of work life and quality of services.

SOURCE: Used with permission of Madeleine Hawn, Executive Director, Gateways, Inc., St. Louis, Missouri.

These indicators are set up on a monthly reporting grid and tracked using specific measures and reporting schedules. For example, Item 7, pertaining to staff turnover, is tracked monthly using turnover data and annualized. This information is compared internally with agency turnover statistics from previous years and externally with turnover data from similar organizations. These data may also be displayed visually, as shown in the hypothetical example in Table 6.3.

STEPS IN DEVELOPING
THE PERFORMANCE MONITORING GRID

To establish a performance monitoring grid for her facility, Carmen will follow these steps:

TABLE 6.3   Hypothetical Monitoring Grid for Performance Indicators

Customer/ Stakeholder Group	Performance Indicators	Measures	Jan.	Feb.	Mar.	Apr.	May	Trends
Residents	1. Abuse and neglect	Reports	1	0	2	0	0	Flat
	2. Safe and healthy environments	Injuries	3	2	5	7	9	Increasing
	3. Personal plan outcomes	% Reached	65	67	66	63	65	Mixed
	4. Satisfaction with programs	% Satisfied	73	74	77	78	79	Increasing
	5. Community supports	% In place	54	55	53	56	55	Flat

1. Determine major customer and stakeholder groups (who do we serve and who benefits from our work or has an interest in it?).

2. Establish key expectations or requirements for each customer or stakeholder group (what our customers/stakeholders need or want from us).

3. Group key expectations by customer or stakeholder type (major families of measures).

4. Express these requirements in outcome terms (end states to achieve).

5. Determine indicators and metrics for each outcome, including desired directions of change (how we will measure progress).

6. Determine reporting intervals for each indicator (how often each one will be measured or tracked).

7. Set up data in a grid or other format (a visual display that makes it easy to track and understand).

8. Establish baseline data (begin with measurements of where we are now).

9. Track data over time and analyze (monitor progress and determine if results are in the desired direction).

10. Continuously evaluate the system for effectiveness (periodically ask the question: Is our system adequate to track major expectations of customer/stakeholder groups?).

Now that Carmen has an understanding of her customers and their expectations, along with a system for tracking progress, how does she organize the facility to seek improvements? That is the focus of the next chapter.

REFERENCES

Daft, R. L. (1992). *Organizational theory and design*. New York: West.

Kotter, J. P., & Heskett, J. L. (1992). *Corporate culture and performance*. New York: Free Press.

Martin, L. L., & Kettner, P. M. (1996). *Measuring the performance of human service programs*. Thousand Oaks, CA: Sage.

Sluyter, G. V., & Martin, M. A. (1996). Measuring the performance of behavioral healthcare organizations: A proposed model. *Best Practices and Benchmarking in Healthcare, 1*(6), 283-289.

Thor, C. G. (1995, Summer). Using a family of measures to assess organizational performance. *National Productivity Review*, pp. 111-131.

CONSTRUCTING THE INFRASTRUCTURE FOR ORGANIZATIONAL IMPROVEMENT

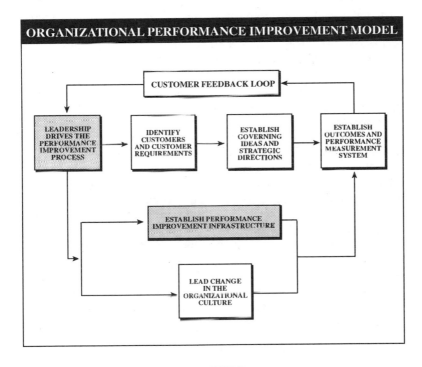

ORGANIZATIONAL PERFORMANCE IMPROVEMENT MODEL

CUSTOMER FEEDBACK LOOP

LEADERSHIP DRIVES THE PERFORMANCE IMPROVEMENT PROCESS → IDENTIFY CUSTOMERS AND CUSTOMER REQUIREMENTS → ESTABLISH GOVERNING IDEAS AND STRATEGIC DIRECTIONS → ESTABLISH OUTCOMES AND PERFORMANCE MEASUREMENT SYSTEM

ESTABLISH PERFORMANCE IMPROVEMENT INFRASTRUCTURE

LEAD CHANGE IN THE ORGANIZATIONAL CULTURE

CHAPTER 7
ESTABLISHING THE INFRASTRUCTURE
FOR PERFORMANCE IMPROVEMENT
*METROPOLITAN CITY CHAPTER
OF NATIONAL CHARITIES, INC.*

Martha Martin, ACSW, was very excited. As Executive Director of the Metropolitan City Chapter of National Charities, Inc., she had finally found a way to empower her employees to get more involved in helping the organization get better!

Martha had just finished reading about a new approach to management called "self-directed work teams." She understood the idea to mean that she should form a number of small work teams throughout the agency, give them a task, and turn the rest over to the team members. They would then set their own guidelines, meeting times, direction, and performance outcomes, later reporting on progress to the administration.

Martha's organization needed some pumping up. She thought that its mission was clear enough, "to help people in need." Her staff included a dedicated group of social workers and other helping professionals. Agency services ran the gamut from running shelters to providing clothing, food, and other basics for people in need, as well as counseling and referral services for people with substance abuse and mental health problems.

The problem, as she saw it, was that the staff had gotten in a rut. Morale was low, people did not seem motivated to do much more than absolutely necessary, and there seemed to be many barriers to change. For instance, the admission process was so cumbersome that people tended to avoid finding new cases. Surely the introduction of empowered work teams would change all that.

Martha called her supervisory staff into her office that afternoon and gave them the basics of her bold new plan. She gave them a list of priorities and told them to form autonomous, self-directed work teams to work on them. Further, she advised them not to interfere with the work of the teams, but to serve only as guides and supporters.

When the supervisors left with their new assignments, Martha sat back in her chair feeling very pleased with herself, so much so that she did not notice her supervisors giving each other furtive and puzzled looks as they left her office.

———————

LEARNING OBJECTIVES

- To discuss the importance of an infrastructure for performance improvement
- To introduce the idea of a Performance Council to oversee the improvement process

- To develop a framework for performance improvement teams
- To review basic elements in the needed support structure

It is highly likely that within a few weeks, Martha will be faced with a rude awakening. Although her approach to performance improvement was good, the deployment of that idea was not sound. The supervisors who went forth to carry out this new approach left Martha's office with more than some concern about the idea. Not only was it given to them without a context, it also may run counter to some of their very deeply held convictions about how to run the agency.

For a higher probability of success, leadership must put into place an infrastructure to help support the performance improvement efforts. This infrastructure has three important components: (a) a structure for change, (b) the development of effective teams, and (c) a support system for success. If any of these three components is missing, the organization will have a very difficult time introducing and sticking with this approach to performance.

STRUCTURE FOR CHANGE

The first of these components is to establish a structure for change. The traditional approach to managing organizational performance, as we have discussed before, too often relies exclusively on an inspection or "quality assurance" approach. Although leaders certainly need to monitor agency processes and outcomes, they must also have a way of applying what they have learned to improving those processes and outcomes.

Several authors in the field of quality management suggest the formation of a special team or standing committee to help monitor and give energy to organizational performance efforts. Juran (1989) calls this group the Quality Council and suggests that its basic responsibility is to "launch, coordinate, and 'institutionalize' annual quality improvement" (p. 43).

I have found that the formation of such an entity is critical to successful application of the approach we have been discussing. The tendency is for organizational leaders to want the quality function kept close at hand, often designating themselves (the executive team) as the primary body responsible for organizational performance. Although this approach has merit, it often falls apart in practice, primarily because of competing demands on the executive group. Crises and other survival or high-visibility issues often push into the background the longer view necessary for successful performance improvement efforts.

In some organizations, the executive group delineates for itself two separate roles, one as the agency's operational authority and one as the Quality Council. To maintain focus on quality and performance issues, the team sets aside a portion of time in each of its regular meetings for those issues. Still, there is a tendency to be distracted by dozens of issues that seem at the time to be more pressing.

Whether the leadership groups elect to serve in both roles or whether they wish to delegate performance oversight to another group, it is helpful to distinguish between the role of the executive team and that of the quality or performance council. Table 7.1 displays such a distinction.

A good approach for organizations new to these ideas is for the executive team to carry out the functions of the Performance Council at the beginning of the process (the first 6 to 12 months), later turning over the performance improvement functions to another group. One or two members of the executive group would continue on the new Performance Improvement Council to maintain the vital link between the two groups.

Membership of the Council should include a broad cross section of the agency, including staff from direct service, support, supervisory, and administrative areas. The optimal size of the group is 7 to 10 people. The Council's major functions include the following:

1. Establishes a proposed Performance Improvement Plan for review and approval by the Executive Team. The plan includes a definition of organizational performance, description of major customers and stakeholders and their expectations, key outcomes and performance measurement indicators, the role and functions of the Council, and details about formation and chartering of performance improvement.

2. Establishes guidelines for formation of performance improvement teams, including elements of the team charter.

3. Obtains input and ideas from customers, employees, and stakeholders regarding performance issues.

4. Determines which issues should be addressed by cross-functional performance improvement teams and develops charters for those teams.

5. Reviews work and recommendations of the performance teams.

6. Reports progress to the executive team, the agency, and its stakeholders.

7. Helps the agency celebrate progress and success.

A detailed Charter is included at the end of this chapter in the Appendix as a guide for the establishment of the Performance Council.

TABLE 7.1 Comparison of Roles: Executive Team and Quality Council

Executive Team	Quality or Performance Council
Establishes mission, vision, and values (governing ideas)	Seeks opportunities for performance improvement within governing ideas
Establishes the agency's strategic plan and the agency policy (with Board)	Identifies improvement issues within the framework of strategic plan
Determines nature of the agency's approach to performance; establishes and communicates top management commitment	Provides leadership and helps carry out the agency's performance mission
Appoints the Quality or Performance Council and oversees its activities	Charters performance improvement teams and reviews their progress
Reports to the agency's Board of Directors and is accountable to the Board for management of the agency	Reports to the Executive Team and is accountable to it for performance improvement efforts
Helps create the organizational climate to support TQM efforts	Helps create the organizational climate to support TQM efforts
Helps recognize employees and teams for successful efforts	Helps recognize employees and teams for successful efforts
Establishes lines of authority and responsibility for the agency	Works within lines of authority and responsibility and negotiates issues that cut across lines of authority
Helps resolve conflicts among staff and serves as final arbiter for disagreements	Helps facilitate communication and tries to negotiate agreements
Develops and maintains agency budget and allocates resources within the agency	No role except setting resource limits for performance improvement teams
Interacts with agency's external environment (marketing, PR, politics)	No role in external environment unless so designated
Establishes employee grievance policy and may be included in step process	No role
Reviews and approves agency performance improvement plan	Proposes performance plan, including guidelines for team formation
Authorizes resources for training and support	Provides training and support to teams as needed

EFFECTIVE TEAM DEVELOPMENT

Many organizational problems can be resolved by an individual manager or other employee working alone. It would be wasteful of resources and frustrating to the organization to form a team for every performance issue needing to be addressed.

Special action teams are particularly useful, however, when the issue is highly complex or requires the special skills of a variety of persons within the organization. For example, one of Martha Martin's concerns is with the admission process for her agency. It had become so cumbersome, unworkable, and aversive over the years that agency employees avoided taking on new clients to avoid having to plow through the system.

This is a fairly complex issue that could very well justify the resources of a cross-functional performance improvement team. Team members might include case managers, supervisors, clinicians who screen referrals, management information staff, clerical staff, and several clients or family members. A skillful team can build on these diverse perspectives on the problem and find new solutions to the problem. A successful and simplified revision of the admission process ultimately would be responsive to the needs of both external customers and employees.

Martha also will be well served to provide her teams with more structure than she originally planned. The use of a team charter is a very useful device for structuring the work of such teams and helps improve their productivity. Charters may be developed by a department head and given to a group of the employees who report directly to him or her. Such teams may involve natural work groups or a special group whose members come from several such natural work groups.

If the focus of the team cuts across several departments or sections, then it should be chartered by the Performance Improvement Council. The charter is a brief and concise written document that includes at least the following elements.

- List of team members (names, position, and key team role);
- Date assigned;
- Mission or problem to be addressed;
- Expected improvements;
- Boundaries and constraints;
- Expected time line;
- Special ground rules;
- Follow-up (if known)

The team charter for Martha's Admission Team might look like the one in Box 7.1. Let me make a few explanatory comments about this team

---

BOX 7.1. *Metropolitan City Chapter of National Charities, Inc., Team Charter*

Team Name: To be determined by the team

Team Members: J. Shimrock, Admissions Coordinator—*Team Leader*
R. Newcomb, Volunteer Coordinator—*Team Facilitator*
M. Hartsing, Billing Supervisor
A. Vanguard, Case Management Supervisor
G. Flood, Substance Abuse Counselor
W. Abercrombie, Client Family Member
J. Beesley, Management Information Specialist

Date Assigned: April 26, 19xx

Problem to Be Addressed: Clients, staff, and stakeholders have long complained about problems with the client admission process. It takes from 4 to 6 weeks to process a new application and admit someone into any of the agency's services. Case managers are reluctant to find new clients because of this cumbersome, unworkable, and aversive process.

Expected Improvements: Study the process from the perspectives of all users and recommend changes that will make it simple, workable, and effective.

Boundaries and Constraints: Team is empowered to collect any data needed. All recommendations will be reviewed by the agency's Executive Team for final decision.

Resources Available: The team may spend up to $250 for data collection, consultation, or other needed resources. Team leader will arrange.

Expected Time Line: A final report and set of recommendations are due within 90 days. Team leader will meet with Performance Council in 45 days to provide preliminary findings.

Special Ground Rules: Team should select its own operating ground rules. Team is advised to consult with other performance teams currently in process (Billing Procedures, Paperwork Reduction, and Organizational Structure).

Follow-Up: Any changes made to the admissions procedures by the Executive Team should be assessed periodically by the team for a period of 1 year to provide feedback on effectiveness.

charter. First of all, notice that two of the team members have been assigned the special roles of *team leader* and *team facilitator*. The team leader directs the activities of the team, sets the agenda, calls the meeting to order, conducts the meeting, and focuses on the *content* or *what is done*. The team facilitator, on the other hand, serves as more of an adviser to the team. He or she assists the team leader with team management, acts as an observer of team dynamics and interactions, intervenes when the team process becomes sticky or unproductive, and generally focuses on *process* or *how things are done*.

Although it is possible for one person to play both roles, my experience is that it is very difficult. The team leader is generally chosen because of his or her special skills and/or interest in the problem at hand. Because of this factor, the team leader generally will become very involved in the content of the team and will have great difficulty shifting focus to process issues.

The team leader and team facilitator act in unison, meeting briefly prior to and after each team meeting to assess progress and to alert each other about any concerns or other issues. During the meeting itself, they should position themselves so as to make easy eye contact with each other in order to stay sensitive to any nonverbal cues that may transmit concerns or questions about the process.

Other roles are assigned by the team itself and may rotate. For example, it is generally desirable to have a timekeeper, scribe, and flip chart recorder. The team leader asks for volunteers for these roles at the end of each meeting along with team discussion about the next agenda.

The section on *boundaries and constraints* is very important to prevent any misunderstandings and hurt feelings. Most of us have worked on one committee or another only to find at the end that we were not actually empowered to make any decisions about the issue. Spelling this issue out clearly helps prevent such problems.

Another point is the section on *special ground rules*. In this case, the team charter advises the team to choose its own operating ground rules. This is an important aspect of effective teams and one of five critical elements suggested by Katzenbach and Smith (1993) of high-performance work teams. The others are a small number of people (less than 12), right mix of complementary skills, commitment to a common purpose and performance goals, and mutual accountability.

Regarding ground rules, I generally present the team with a list of common guidelines and suggest that they discuss them and choose those or any others that they want to adopt. Following are some typical ground rules used by teams:

- Attend all meetings and be on time; notify team leader if emergencies prevent attendance.

- Begin and end all meetings on time unless team agrees to a revised meeting schedule.

- Check your status and rank at the door.

- Listen to and respect the contributions of all members.

- Try to reach decisions through consensus; use voting or majority rule only as a fallback strategy.

- Adopt the "100 mile rule" (take no phone calls or messages that you would not take if you were more than 100 miles from the office).

- Criticize only ideas, not people.

- Use a "parking lot" for ideas that are not germane to the meeting agenda; revisit and dispose of all parking lot ideas prior to the end of the meeting.

- Share the housekeeping tasks with other members (e.g., coffee and refreshments, taking notes, making copies).

- Any member may choose not to speak but agrees that that choice represents his or her response.

- Help the team celebrate success!

I suggest to teams that they write up their final list of ground rules on a page of a flip chart and tape it up in front of the group at the beginning of every meeting as a reminder of the agreement that has been made about a common operating approach. The use of agreed-upon ground rules helps improve the effectiveness of a team (or any work group) considerably. The list can be revised at any time by mutual consent of the team members.

Performance improvement teams can take on literally any problem or issue that acts as a barrier to the organization's best efforts for its customers, employees, or stakeholders. I have collected some examples, shown in Table 7.2, of issues around which such teams have been formed in a variety of mental health organizations with which I have worked.

When organizations are new at this process, I generally give them a few suggestions about the use of performance improvement teams.

1. Teams that function within the confines of a department or section and that work on problems and issues within the purview of that department need not be "officially" sanctioned or chartered by the Performance Improvement Council. They should, however, advise the Council of their work.

2. The roles of team leader and team facilitator for cross-functional teams should be assigned by the Performance Council and should remain the same for the life of the team to ensure continuity.

TABLE 7.2   Selected Performance Improvement Projects From Mental Health
Organizations

Reducing in nursing overtime
Census count accuracy improvement
Improving housekeeping services
Streamlining purchasing process
Reducing client elopements
Reducing workers' compensation costs
Improving employee recognition system
Landscape improvements
Streamlining food delivery
Paperwork reduction
Improving staff development program
Improving personnel selection and retention
Preventing client abuse
Improving the receptionist area
Expanding emergency prevention unit
Reducing medication errors
Streamlining accounting procedures
Improving maintenance response system
Improving consumer application/admission process
Increasing in-home services
Reducing consumer waiting
Reducing treatment plan deficiencies
Reducing staff overtime
Improving information/communication system
Revising facility newsletter

3. Team leaders/facilitators should be given some special training to help
   prepare them for the role. Typically, I provide a 2-day training for team
   leader/facilitators that includes a discussion of team formation and dynamics, roles and structures of teams, quality improvement tools such as
   flowcharting and cause-and-effect diagrams, some hands-on practice, and
   a case study exercise.

4. Team members for cross-functional teams should also be assigned by the
   Council after consultation with the prospective member's immediate supervisor and only with the consent of the member.

5. The Council should invite the team leader and facilitator into a meeting at
   the halfway point to discuss progress and address any problems that may
   have arisen. Sometimes it is necessary to renegotiate the time line or scope
   of the project.

6. Begin with relatively simple projects and issues that have a high probability
   of success and build on that experience. Never begin assigning teams, for
   example, with topics like "world peace."

A SUPPORT SYSTEM
FOR SUCCESS

The third essential component of the infrastructure is the presence of a system that supports performance improvement efforts. The support system must include, at the very minimum, training for all employees and a *supervisory system* that encourages change and facilitates employee empowerment.

Regarding training, the organization must provide for or arrange special training for all employees in the basics of the new performance improvement system. At the minimum, this includes some basic awareness or orientation training for all employees. One approach I have found to be effective is a 3-hour overview seminar that includes the basic concepts and assumptions of quality management, a videotape that shows the application of these principles to a health care or human services organization, and a hands-on team exercise. Although this training can be imported at first via consultants, it should gradually be taken over by in-house trainers to maintain continuity over time because of organizational changes and staff turnover.

At the next level, I suggest some specialized training for those staff members who will adopt the roles of team leader or team facilitator, discussed briefly above. In addition, the organization may offer advanced classes in the use of more complex quality tools, statistical analysis, and the development of effective surveys.

I also suggest that the facility sponsor a half-day refresher or review session for all team leaders and facilitators several times a year to review the concepts and tools learned previously, share experiences, and learn new skills. It is also helpful to sponsor special graduation ceremonies with appropriate pomp and circumstance for graduates of these training events.

Organizations vary greatly with respect to the amount of specialized training in performance improvement areas they provide employees. One recent winner of the Missouri Quality Award (St. Francis Hospital, St. Joseph, Missouri), offers the following in-house training courses for its staff: Basic Concepts of CQI, Team Member Training, Managing Quality Improvement, Team Leader Training, Administrative Council Training, and Facilitator Training (Missouri Quality Award and St. Francis Hospital and Health Services, 1966).

Specialized training also is needed for people in supervisory roles. As employees become members of performance improvement teams and more involved in the overall organizational change process, the role of supervisor changes dramatically. A command, control, and compliance approach is inconsistent with a team-based culture. Each supervisor must become more of a coach, mentor, and facilitator than an overseer.

Some of the new skills needed for effective supervision in the new culture include the development of high-performance work teams, improved communication skills (including listening), coaching, conflict management, providing corrective feedback, giving praise and recognition, and providing new approaches to employee performance evaluation. I try to help people develop these skills through an 18-contact-hour course on basic supervision. However it is done, it is critical that the organization help prepare its supervisors for their new roles.

There are other aspects of a supportive infrastructure for performance improvement, including good management information and communication systems, the organizational structure itself, an adequate fiscal management system, employee wellness programs, and user-friendly human resources systems. Because each of those could turn into a book itself, and because there are many other references in those areas, I have limited my discussion to those infrastructure issues with which I have had the most experience.

The next chapter provides a detailed example of a performance improvement team as it studies the issue of absenteeism in a state psychiatric facility and recommends specific improvements to address the problem.

APPENDIX

CENTERVILLE COMMUNITY MENTAL HEALTH CENTER
SAMPLE PERFORMANCE IMPROVEMENT COUNCIL CHARTER

I. *Mission:* The mission of the Centerville CMHC Performance Improvement Council is to provide direction, guidance, and support for the Center's performance improvement efforts.

II. *Formation:* The Performance Improvement Council is a creation of and accountable to the Center's Executive Committee (Executive Director and direct reports).

III. *Composition:* The Council is composed of two (2) members of the Center's Executive Committee, one (1) representative from each of the Center's program and administrative divisions, one (1) client or client representative, and two (2) other staff members chosen by the nonsupervisory employees of the Center.

IV. *Appointments:* All members of the Council will serve in 1-year staggered terms. Members may not serve successive terms but may be appointed or elected to the Council after 1 year of absence.

V. *Roles:* The specific roles of the Performance Improvement Council are to:

1. Provide direction for the Center's performance improvement efforts by establishing a performance plan for the organization. This plan identifies the Center's customers and stakeholders, performance outcomes or goals, methods for measuring performance, how special teams will function, and how to celebrate success.

2. Establish communication channels to obtain suggestions for performance improvement projects from staff members, clients, parents, and other interested persons and for reporting on accomplishments.

3. Determine specific issues or targets for the establishment of performance improvement teams.

4. Formally charter cross-functional teams and support efforts of chartered teams as well as informal or departmental teams, and document progress.

5. Within the resources provided by the Executive Committee, provide or arrange staff training in quality issues, team leading and facilitation, and in other areas as needed. When resources are not readily available, advocate and lobby for the necessary training services.

6. Review recommendations from quality improvement teams and assist with the implementation of quality improvements.

VI. *Obtaining Input:* The Council obtains ideas and suggestions for the formation of performance improvement teams in the following ways:
   1. The Executive Committee submits ideas and suggestions.
   2. Performance Council members identify issues and make suggestions.
   3. Employees submit ideas through suggestion boxes or supervisors, or during the "quality idea forum" at the end of each Council meeting.
   4. The Council obtains ideas from reviews of external surveys (Medicaid, accreditation, customer surveys, complaints, etc.) and from internal surveys (employee satisfaction surveys, etc.).

VII. *Decision Rules:* It is the responsibility of the Council to determine which issues shall form the basis for chartering quality improvement teams. When possible, the Council should follow these decision criteria when selecting potential projects. (These suggestions for decision criteria are based on ideas from Albrecht, 1992; Jablonski, 1992; and personal communication from John E. Barnette, Shawnee Hills, Inc., Charleston, West Virginia.)
   1. Issues that are relevant to the Center's stated mission, vision, and values
   2. Issues that address quality of services for clients or quality of work life for employees
   3. Areas of extreme customer dissatisfaction (any group of customers)
   4. Areas or processes that cause high employee frustration
   5. Issues that would result in positive and visible change for all or most customers and employees
   6. Chronic problems or issues (things that keep coming back to the table)
   7. Issues that would increase employee discretion or empowerment with little risk or debate about appropriateness
   8. Issues that promise at least 50% probability of being able to be improved by the formation of a quality team

VIII. *Decision Options:* When reviewing ideas for improving the quality of services or the quality of work life, the Council has at least the following options:
   1. Charter a performance improvement team to address the issue *or*
   2. Determine that the issue does not fall within the purview of the Council and refer it to an appropriate level of the organization for follow-up (e.g., Executive Committee, Division Director, Program Director, employee grievance process) *or*
   3. Determine that the idea is appropriate for a quality team but defer action until a more appropriate time.

IX. *Reports:* Team leaders of each performance improvement team chartered by the Council shall meet with the full Council at the halfway mark of their time line to make a preliminary report, request assistance, and/or make any mid-course corrections. In addition, when its work is completed, the full team will meet with the Council to make a final report and recommendations and to celebrate success.

The Council will determine an appropriate mechanism to report and update the organization and its external customers on the progress of the quality teams. The Council will make a formal report to the Executive Committee on its actions at least twice a year.

X. *Team Charters:* The Council will develop guidelines for the team that specify how team members are appointed, the problem to be addressed, expected improvements, resources available, special guidelines and limitations, and any follow-up needed.

XI. *Training and Support:* As a part of its annual plan, the Council will outline the types of training and support needed by performance improvement teams for successful operation.

XII. *Conflict Resolution:* The Council will operate as a model for performance improvement teams, following a structured meeting format and operating by consensus decision making and the adoption of other ground rules by mutual consent.

Within this framework, it is expected that members of the Council will be able to resolve conflicts and differences of opinion. In the event that the Council cannot satisfactorily resolve any given issue, the question may be referred to the Executive Committee for a determination. The decision of the Executive Committee shall be final.

XIII. *Celebration:* The Council helps the organization celebrate success of performance improvement efforts in formal and informal ways, not limited to an annual "Quality Fair" in which each team demonstrates its success in improving organizational performance.

Chartered this ___ day of ____, 19__ by the Center's Executive Committee:

_____   _____
Executive Director   Assistant Director for Finance

_____   _____
Assistant Director for Treatment   Assistant Director, Public Information

_____
Assistant Director, Human Resources

REFERENCES

Albrecht, K. (1992). *The only thing that matters: Bringing the power of the customer into the center of your business.* New York: HarperBusiness.

Jablonski, J. R. (1992). *Implementing TQM: Competing in the nineties through Total Quality Management.* San Diego: Pfeiffer & Company.

Juran, J. M. (1989). *Juran on leadership for quality: An executive handbook.* New York: Free Press.

Katzenbach, J. R., & Smith, D. K. (1993). *The wisdom of teams: Creating the high-performance organization.* New York: HarperBusiness.

Missouri Quality Award and St. Francis Hospital and Health Services. (1996). *1996 Award Recipient Application summary.* Jefferson City: Excellence in Missouri Foundation.

Chapter 8

INTEGRATING THE TOOLS AND TECHNIQUES OF PERFORMANCE IMPROVEMENT
Case Study

ABSENTEEISM AT CENTRAL STATE MENTAL HEALTH CENTER

The Central State Mental Health Center is a state-operated mental health facility, designed to provide inpatient treatment of adult patients with acute psychiatric disorders. The facility accommodates a total of 100 patients on four wards when at full capacity, 25 patients per ward.

Staffing on each ward consists of four full-time on-duty psychiatric aides for both the day and the evening shift, and three psychiatric aides for the night shift. One Registered Nurse Supervisor is assigned to each shift for each ward. For full 24-hour-a-day, 7-day-a-week coverage, there are a total of 51 psychiatric aides and 16 FTE registered nurses.

A review of personnel records shows that absenteeism and turnover rates are very high for this facility, about twice the rate of comparable state inpatient centers. This condition creates a pressure to place new, untrained aides on the job before they have completed their new employee orientation training. Injury rates for both staff and patients also are high.

RNs feel that they have their hands full with the acuity level of patients and are unable to give much personal attention to the psychiatric aides. Their time is eroded by an ever-increasing amount of paperwork, external accreditation reviews, and other demands. This is also true, to some extent, for the aides.

Each ward is of a fairly modern design, with an open nursing station, but has few homelike characteristics. Besides the bedroom areas, there is one large, sterile dayroom and a smaller space for recreational activities. Outside recreation is limited because of the Mental Health Center's inner-city location and lack of outside grounds.

Most of the patients attend activity or work programs off the wards at various intervals during the weekdays, but there seem to be several hours of "dead time" for each of them every day. The weekends are especially bad, and most staff dread pulling weekend shifts. A high percentage of the patients exhibit severe behavioral problems, usually at unpredictable intervals.

The aides' major duties during a given shift include assisting with patients' personal care (bathing, dressing, hygiene), activities of daily living, recreational activities, and dressing, along with record keeping. Because of staff ratios, they generally have to work alone and may have difficulty getting away for breaks.

Most of the psychiatric aides' work tasks are highly structured by the policy manual, an imposing volume put out by the Mental Health Center's administration. In addition to the policy manual and its strict enforcement by the RN Supervisors, aides find themselves bombarded by a constant stream of demands from other personnel, including psychiatrists, psychologists, social workers, recreation therapists, and occupational therapists. Sometimes they are confused by conflicting orders and do not always feel that their supervisors will back them in a conflict with other personnel. Aides are generally not included in treatment team meetings.

The Mental Health Center's management is very concerned about the facility's high injury rates, high absenteeism, and high turnover rates for psychiatric aides. The center's Performance Improvement Council has chartered a team to study the high absenteeism, determine major causes for this situation, and recommend corrective action to help resolve the problem.

LEARNING OBJECTIVES

- To provide readers with the opportunity to integrate the tools and techniques of performance improvement through a case study
- To introduce the use of several major performance improvement tools
- To demonstrate a performance improvement team process

The Central State Mental Health Center has a serious absenteeism problem among its direct service staff. The quality of care is in jeopardy, as are staff and patients. The organization's Performance Improvement Council has chartered a Performance Improvement Team to study the problem and recommend solutions. The Council begins by issuing the team charter shown in Box 8.1.

BOX 8.1. *Central State Mental Health Center Team Charter*

Team Name: To be determined by the team

Team Members: Art Monroe, Assistant Superintendent for Treatment, Team Leader

Cheryl Riggins, Quality Improvement Coordinator, Team Facilitator

Janet Hawn, Director of Nursing

Bill Miller, Director of Training

Carl Jones, Psychiatric Aide, Evening Shift

Maria Gonzalez, Shift Supervisor

Bobbie Sylvia, Human Resources Technician

Date Assigned: June 5, 19xx

Problem to Be Addressed: The facility is experiencing high absenteeism rates for the psychiatric aides, about twice the rates of comparable mental health facilities in the state. This is causing understaffing, poor-quality patient services, dangerous client and staff environments, and high turnover rates for many categories of staff. It is also placing the facility's Joint Commission Accreditation status in jeopardy.

Expected Improvements: Using a team approach and quality management tools, the team should study the problem in depth, determine the major root causes of high absenteeism, and recommend workable solutions for review by the Performance Improvement Council and Executive Team.

Boundaries and Constraints: The team is empowered to review relevant data as it is made available. Teams should strive to use consensus decision-making strategies. Recommendations will be reviewed by the Performance Improvement Council and sent on to the Executive Team for final decisions on implementation. The team should make its best recommendations based on whatever conclusions it may draw from the analysis, irrespective of the potential cost of improvements.

BOX 8.1 *(continued)*

Resources Available: The team has access to technical staff in the Quality Improvement Department and a consultant from the Community College. In addition, the team may use whatever data collection methods it chooses, including surveys, focus groups, benchmarking, and the facility's management information system. The team leader will make arrangements for needed resources.

Expected Timeline: The team should complete its work and make its recommendations to the Performance Improvement Council within 90 days. The team leader and facilitator should meet with the Performance Improvement Council in 45 days to discuss progress and concerns.

Special Ground Rules: None

Follow-Up: The team should consider implementing several pilot efforts that can be monitored periodically over the next year to determine effectiveness. The team should reconvene as needed throughout the year to review progress and report same to the Performance Improvement Council.

TEAM MEETING #1—9:00 A.M., JUNE 12, ADMINISTRATIVE CONFERENCE ROOM A

A. Monroe: Thank you all for coming and for agreeing to be a part of this performance improvement team. I think we all agree that the high absenteeism rate is affecting the facility's ability to provide quality services for our patients and is having a negative impact on our staff.

J. Hawn: Hear, hear! That is an understatement!

Team: (Sounds of general assent around the table)

A. Monroe: I appreciate the sentiments. Jan and I hope that we can show some real progress toward improving the situation. Cheryl will be our team facilitator throughout the team process, and as we learned in our training, we will rotate the timekeeper, recorder, and other roles. Could I have a volunteer for timekeeper for this meeting?

B. Miller: I'll take it today, Art.

A. Monroe: Thanks, Bill. We have about an hour for this preliminary meeting and the agenda is posted. Today we need to review and adopt our ground rules, read and understand the team charter, and lay out a work schedule on a Gantt chart. I suggest we begin by having each of you introduce yourselves and tell us a little bit about your perspective on the issue. Give us a sign at the 15-minute mark, Bill, and we will see where we are at that time. So, who would like to begin?

M. Gonzalez: I'd like to start. I am Maria Gonzalez, Shift Supervisor on Ward, A and I have been here for 15 years. In all this time I have never seen it to be a worse situation. We just . . .

Team: (Team continues discussion for the next 15 minutes. Some of the comments included during this session include the following:

You know, our staff here at Central State have a reputation throughout the state mental health system as being lazy and uncommitted. I don't necessarily agree. I wonder if this perception has any impact on the problem?

I have noted that the RN Supervisors on all wards seem to always be very busy because of paperwork and other busywork and are unavailable to help the psychiatric aides with patient problems.

I'm told that some of the psychiatric aides are heavy drinkers and have been at local bars between 2:00 and 3:00 in the morning. I wonder how many call in sick because of hangovers?

A group of psychiatric aides has been meeting secretly during their breaks. I have hard that they agree among themselves to be absent from work sometimes as a group to go to the beach or someplace.

Some people say that the aides do not treat housekeeping staff very well, which causes high turnover among that group.

More than once, I have seen psychiatric aides at shopping malls during their regular shifts.

It is common knowledge that the highest absentecism rates occur on Mondays.

A lot of supervisors around here think that the best way to reduce absenteeism among aides is simply to increase the punishment for failing to come to work for any reason.

A. Monroe: OK, team, thanks for that introduction. This will be helpful as we begin to search for root causes for the problem. I want to remind us all, however, that as we learned in training, some of the information we have about a problem is more reliable than other information. We will need to work to sort out those things that are valid and those that are the result of rumor and guesswork. Our job is to validate what we know or think we know and to obtain other data to help us with the task at hand.

Before we go any further into the content, however, I want to see if we can agree on a set of ground rules for the team. If you would look at your handout packet, you will find a set of proposed ground rules. I would appreciate it if each member would read one and then let's discuss and clarify. Bill, give us 20 minutes for this one. Bobbie, would you read the first one?

B. Sylvia: Sure, Art. "Attend all meetings and be on time."

A. Monroe: Any questions or comments?

J. Hawn: Yeah. . . . I wonder what we do in case of emergencies. Sometimes, I get a call regarding a patient crisis that I have to attend to and might be late even with the best of intentions.

C. Riggins: I think we are all faced with that kind of situation. Some teams I have facilitated modify the statement slightly to read, "Attend all meetings and be on time. In case of an emergency, member will notify team leader." This way we can agree to the ground rule but recognize legitimate exceptions.

Team: (General assent)

(The team continues with this process until all ground rules have been read and discussed)

A. Monroe: Thanks, team. Well, we have read and discussed this list of ground rules. What would you like to do?

B. Sylvia: These look pretty good to me and are similar to the list that we reviewed in training. I'd like to add that we agree to keep the process part of our meetings confidential.

B. Miller: I'm not sure we can do that. This isn't client information, and we have an open meetings law in the state.

B. Sylvia: I didn't mean that this should apply to the content of our work, just the process. In other words, we talk about *what* we are accomplishing, but not the blow by blow interactions, etc.

B. Miller: In that case, I think we would be OK.

(After some more discussion, the team agrees to a set of ground rules, and Cheryl agrees to type them up on a card for each member and place them on a flip chart to be attached to the wall before each meeting as a reminder)

A. Monroe: OK, we are making progress and staying in the time lines for the agenda. Let's move now to a careful review of the team charter. You have a copy in your folders. Carl, would you begin by reading the problem to be addressed? I suggest that we discuss each section until we are sure that everyone understands what is expected of us.

C. Jones: OK, "Problem to Be Addressed: The facility is experiencing high absenteeism rates . . ."

(Team moves on through the charter and discusses each section. There are a few questions that need clarification from the Performance Improvement Council. A. Monroe agrees to find out and report back at the next meeting. The team also makes some suggestions about data collection efforts and identifies several specific action items)

A. Monroe: All right, we have made a good start today. We have gotten to know each other a bit, reviewed each other's perspectives on the problem, adopted a set of ground rules, studied and clarified the team charter, and suggested some beginning action items. Now we can begin digging into the problem at the next meeting. I suggest the following for the agenda.

1. Ask the Performance Improvement Council to clarify the questions raised and bring back answers (A. Monroe).

2. Bring in absenteeism data for the most recent month, to be reviewed by the team (B. Sylvia).

3. Discuss whatever additional information members can discover on their own before the next meeting, based on informal interviews or other data (all team members).

4. Begin the development of a survey instrument to determine why aides stay home from their perspective (all team members).

5. Discuss specific improvement goals. I am thinking about some kind of target for absenteeism reduction, say 25% reduction within one year. Anything else?

C. Riggins: I'd like to bring in Dr. Joe Schimock, our consultant from the Community College, to give us a briefing on how to develop a good survey. I think it will help us to get better results in the long run.

A. Monroe: Any objections?

Team: (General assent)

A. Monroe: Then that will be our agenda. I will have it typed up and distributed to each of you prior to our next meeting. As we agreed earlier, we will meet at this time and in this place for an hour each week. Before we adjourn, we have about 5 minutes left and I would like to ask Cheryl to help us with a brief evaluation of our meeting. Cheryl?

C. Riggins: If you remember from training, we know that one way to help teams get better is for them to evaluate each of their meetings so that any changes can be made. We could use a formal evaluation tool such as the one in your folder or an informal one. Usually, I suggest that teams use the formal tool about once a month and do an informal one each time. Would that be OK?

Team: (General assent)

C. Riggins: OK, then let me ask you to share with us some of the things you liked about today's meeting, and some things that you think we can improve on. I will put your comments into two columns here on the flip chart.

(After this informal evaluation, the team adjourned right on time)

TEAM MEETING #2—9:00 A.M., JUNE 19,
ADMINISTRATIVE CONFERENCE ROOM

At this meeting, the team proceeds with the agenda decided on last time. Art Monroe reports on the answers he got from the Performance Improvement Council. The team discusses a target for reduction of absenteeism but decides it cannot set a goal until it has a better feel for the extent of the problem. The team then begins the process of reviewing absenteeism data brought in by B. Sylvia. These data are displayed in Table 8.1.

After looking over the data, the team agrees to display it in the form of a run chart. The run chart, shown in Figure 8.1, provides a visual picture of trends in the data over time. (Further information on how to develop a run chart is contained in the "Performance Improvement Tool Kit" in Chapter 9.)

Based on the analysis of these data, the team reached the obvious conclusion that most of the facility's absenteeism problem occurs on the weekends, contrary to the conventional wisdom that it happened on Mondays. Some other information picked up by team members over the course of the previous week lends credence to a growing theory that there are some serious problems on the weekends. Here are some of the things that team members found out:

1. New psychiatric aides are generally assigned to weekends and holidays.
2. Supervision is decreased on weekends because of other duties assigned.
3. Therapy and rehabilitation programs do not operate on the weekends except for a skeleton recreation program.
4. Professional staff are not readily available on weekends, holidays, or evenings, except on call for extreme emergencies.
5. Housekeeping services are not available on weekends except for a roving crew of two persons for emergencies.
6. The laundry closes at 5:00 p.m. on Fridays.
7. Only one social worker is available for the entire campus on weekends and holidays.
8. Psychiatric aides do not receive adequate training until they have been on the job for six months.
9. It generally takes six weeks to fill a psychiatric aide vacancy.
10. There is no specific training program for supervisory staff.
11. The new employee orientation program takes 1 week to complete and has not been revised for 8 years.
12. Sunday, April 15, was Easter.

TABLE 8.1   Central State Mental Health Center Absenteeism Data for Psychiatric Aides (April, 19xx)

Day of the Week	Total Number of Aides Absent (All Shifts)
Sunday	25
Monday	14
Tuesday	10
Wednesday	8
Thursday	7
Friday	7
Saturday	20
Sunday	22
Monday	10
Tuesday	11
Wednesday	8
Thursday	9
Friday	10
Saturday	12
Sunday	36
Monday	8
Tuesday	10
Wednesday	4
Thursday	12
Friday	9
Saturday	22
Sunday	24
Monday	8
Tuesday	10
Wednesday	11
Thursday	9
Friday	8
Saturday	18
Sunday	23
Monday	8

Average number of aides absent per day = 13.1; standard deviation = 7.28

Based on this information, the team began to form some preliminary conclusions about causes of the absenteeism problem and sorted them into several major clusters or groupings: weekend inadequacies (programmatic and administrative), training issues, problems with the hiring process, and a lack of professional support for aide staff.

The team agreed, however, not to risk reaching premature conclusions until some additional data could be collected. This discussion led to a

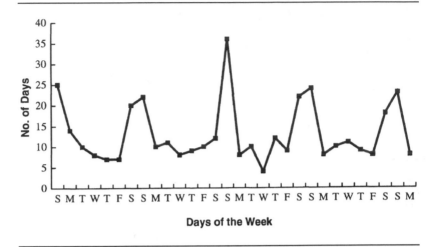

Figure 8.1. *Run Chart for Absenteeism Data, Month of April*

decision to develop a survey of reasons why aides are absent from *their* point of view. A subgroup of three members was assigned the task of developing a list of potential questions for the survey for review by the team.

Because the team decided early on to meet only once a week for one hour, it took several weeks before the survey was completed, administered to the psychiatric aides, and analyzed. When the data were in, the team constructed a Pareto Chart to get a visual picture of the major causes of absenteeism as reported by aides. This chart is shown in Figure 8.2. (Information on how to develop and use a Pareto Chart is contained in the "Performance Improvement Tool Kit" in Chapter 9.)

Based on their review of the Pareto Chart, the team determined that about 80% of the absenteeism problem seemed to stem from four major causes: The perception of not getting enough help or support from aide supervisors; no help with behavior problems of clients, especially on weekends; insufficient client programs, particularly on weekends; and the resulting stress and burnout.

These findings added weight to information already gathered about the impact of weekend issues on absenteeism. In addition, it highlighted concerns about the quality and availability of supervision.

During this time, the team also decided to construct a flowchart of the hiring process and assigned that task to another subgroup. This allowed

Responses to Survey Questions	# Responses	% of Total
Not enough client programs, especially on weekends	31	16.1
Too many people giving us orders	3	1.6
No recognition or appreciation for a job well done	14	7.3
Not enough help or support from supervisors	41	21.4
Not enough training for the job	18	9.4
Family emergencies that prevent us from coming to work	10	5.2
Second job conflicts with work schedule	7	3.7
Sometimes just need a "mental health day"	5	2.6
Need more help with behavior problems, especially weekends	36	18.8
We feel stressed and "burned out" most of the time	27	14.1

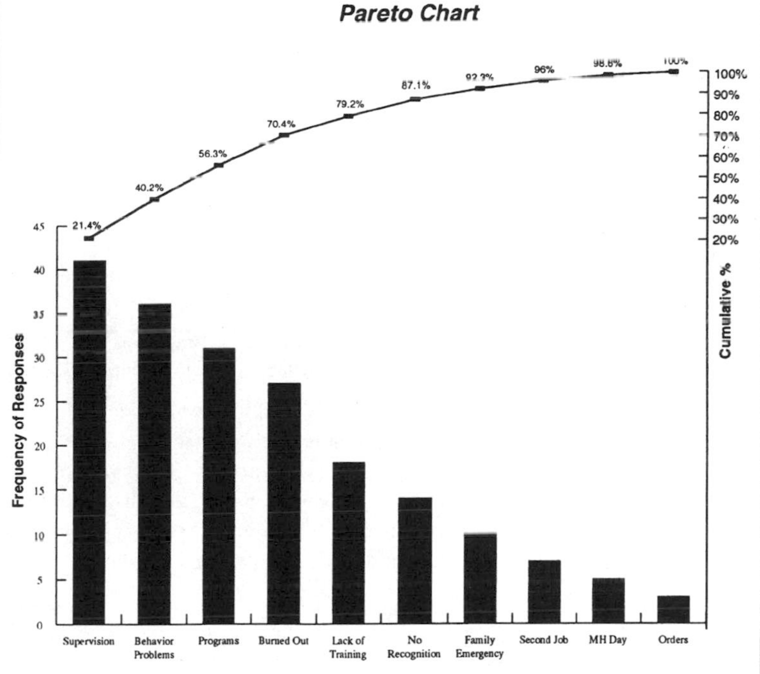

Figure 8.2. *Central State Mental Health Center Survey of Psychiatric Aides: "Why Do You Stay Home?"*

each of the subgroups to be able to work in a parallel fashion and helped the team to make better use of its time. (Information on how to develop and use a flowchart is contained in the "Performance Improvement Tool Kit" in Chapter 9.)

TEAM MEETING #6—9:00 A.M., AUGUST 31, ADMINISTRATIVE CONFERENCE ROOM

A. Monroe: Welcome back, team. I am impressed with the progress we have made in just a few short weeks and want to compliment each of you on your participation in this process. I think we are getting close to having a pretty good idea about what's at the bottom of our high absenteeism rates.

M. Gonzalez: Yes, this place is being run like a day care center!

A. Monroe: There is a lot to that, Maria. It does appear that the Center is not paying much attention to weekend and holiday coverage and programming. Because we are a 7-day-a-week, 24-hour-a-day operation, this is causing a lot of problems.

J. Hawn: I am worried that we are going to begin stepping on some toes around here if we start making unpopular suggestions like increased staffing on the weekends. I don't think administration will like that one!

A. Monroe: I appreciate your concerns, Jan, and guess that there is always that risk when a team recommends some difficult or unpopular ideas.

(Team members begin chiming in on the discussion)

A. Monroe: Excuse me. Forgive me for interrupting the conversation, but we do have a very heavy agenda this morning. Since we don't want to go overtime, could I suggest that we put that discussion in the parking lot until we get to the recommendations? We still have some data to generate and analyze before we get there.

Team (General assent)

A. Monroe: OK, thanks. Our agenda today is to complete the flowchart of the hiring process for psychiatric aides. Based on the data we have collected so far, we know that our process impedes our ability to get new people on the wards in a timely fashion. That, in turn, causes coverage problems, increases stress, leads to injuries and accidents, and, of course, absenteeism among the aides scheduled to be on duty.

Until we thoroughly understand the current process, of course, we can't make any informed changes. Let's take a look at the steps in the process of filling vacancies, as we have received from the Human Resources Department.

(The team reviews the sequence of steps listed in Box 8.2)

BOX 8.2. *Central State Mental Health*

CENTER PROCESS FOR FILLING VACANCIES OF PSYCHIATRIC AIDES

Nurse supervisor sends a request for hiring (Form HR-100) to Human Resources.

Form HR-100 is date-stamped and placed in a file along with new hire requests in order or receipt.

Personnel clerk reviews all new orders on Monday mornings.

Personnel clerk decides if a vacancy notice must be posted in the local newspaper.

If a posting is necessary, clerk notifies the business office with request for a purchase order for payment of the advertisement.

Business office determines if money is available for the advertisement.

If money is available, an approval form is completed and returned to the clerk.

If no money is available, request for purchase order is rejected and returned to the clerk within 7 days.

If advertisement is approved, the clerk writes the ad and sends it by mail to the local newspaper.

Applications are received in the HR department, stamped by date received, and reviewed in order of receipt.

A panel of three employees reviews all applications for completeness and eligibility.

Applicants who meet minimum specifications are placed on a list for interview.

A letter is sent out to those applicants to schedule interviews.

Applicants are interviewed only on the second Thursday of the month

Those selected are processed through the HR office on the first of the following month.

Those hired are sent to new employee orientation (7-day orientation) which is held once a month during the third week of the month.

Those who successfully complete orientation are sent to the floor to report to work.

If applicant does not complete orientation, his or her employment is terminated within the probationary period.

Using this information, the team begins to develop a flowchart that provides a picture of the process. This is a tedious and time-consuming process. At the end of the hour, the team is only partially finished. Two members agree to take what has been done and work on it prior to the next meeting.

TEAM MEETING #7—9:00 A.M., SEPTEMBER 7, ADMINISTRATIVE CONFERENCE ROOM

At this meeting, the team reviews a flowchart of the hiring process, which has been prepared by the subgroup. The finished product is displayed in Figure 8.3. (Information on how to construct a flowchart is contained in the "Performance Improvement Tool Kit" located in Chapter 9.)

B. Sylvia: Welcome back. Art is ill this week, so I will be filling in as team leader. Our agenda is to review the flowchart provided by the subgroup and reach some conclusions about how to improve and simplify the process. Jan, would you walk us through your flowchart?

The team members review and discuss the flowchart, revising and refining as they go along. Based on this analysis, the team identifies several points in the process that could be streamlined or eliminated to reduce the time for hiring new staff. The team then adjourns and agrees that the next meeting will be devoted to beginning the development of a cause-and-effect or fishbone diagram.

At the next meeting, the team begins to isolate the major factors that appear to be at the root cause of the Center's absenteeism problem. After looking over all the data, they agree on the following major areas: supervision, insufficient support, personnel, and training. After clustering all the various possible causes into these four categories, the team constructs the fishbone diagram shown in Figure 8.4. (Information on how to construct a cause-and-effect diagram is contained in the "Performance Improvement Tool Kit" located in Chapter 9.)

FINAL TEAM MEETING—9:00 A.M., DECEMBER 1, ADMINISTRATIVE CONFERENCE ROOM A

A. Monroe: Well, folks, we are about at the end of our journey together, at least with this issue. I want to thank each of you for your good work

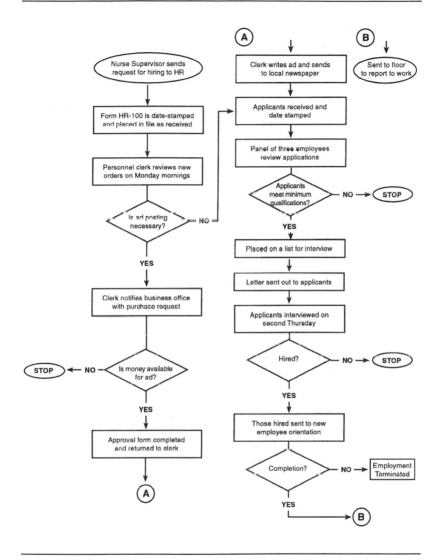

Figure 8.3. *Flowchart of the Hiring Process*

and participation. I think you have done a great job collecting and analyzing the data and in isolating the major causes of the absenteeism problem. Now we need to come up with some recommendations that we think will have an impact.

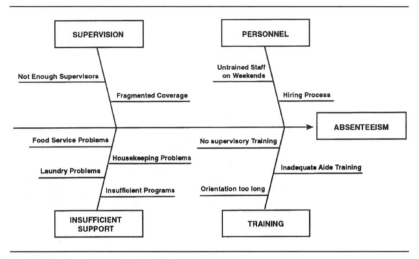

Figure 8.4. *Cause-and-Effect Diagram*

	As we agreed earlier, we hope that these ideas will lead to at least a 25% reduction in absenteeism, a 50% reduction in client injuries, and a 30% reduction in employee turnover. If we can help accomplish only one of those goals, we have made a real contribution. Any questions?
Team:	(Group—nods all around)
J. Hawn:	No, let's get it done.
A. Monroe:	OK, team, let me ask you a general question. We will look at all the data we have collected and analyzed as we develop our recommendations, but what is your general sense of what the core of the problem is?
B. Sylvia:	Well, I'll tell you. It looks to me like this place is being operated as a 5-day-a-week, 8-hour-a-day program, rather than a 24-hour-a-day, 365-day-a-year operation. That's where we need to start.

The team continued the discussion until each member gave his or her perspective. Then, looking at the fishbone diagram, the team developed a number of possible recommendations to help reduce absenteeism. After further discussion, they agreed to the following:

1. Establish a systemwide policy regarding minimum staffing ratios for client and staff security.

2. Obtain funding needed to hire additional staff if needed, including part-time, on-call staff to maintain staffing ratios.

3. Streamline the hiring process to reduce the time to replace aides on the wards—we suggest that reductions of up to 5 days can be achieved through restructuring of the process.

4. Assign professional staff coverage on the weekends on a rotating basis, including an Office of the Day rotation for all administrative staff.

5. Provide supervisors with additional training.

6. Cease the practice of placing newly hired aides on the weekends unless sufficient backup is in place.

7. Increase training for aides in proper and safe handling of aggressive client behaviors.

8. Restructure the schedule for food service, housekeeping, and maintenance to provide better weekend coverage.

9. Establish stress management programs for staff.

10. Increase formal and informal staff recognition programs.

The team's recommendations were then sent on the Performance Council, which reviewed them and agreed to move forward to implement the majority of them. The team was called back in at periodic intervals to assess the impact of their suggestions. Within a year, the absenteeism rate among aides had dropped by 17%, the client injury rates by 65%, and turnover by 28%, clearly indicating a successful effort.

Chapter 9

REFERENCES AND RESOURCES

Fortunately for the practitioner, there is a wealth of information on various aspects of performance improvement or quality management. Although much of it is geared to private sector manufacturing organizations, there is a growing body of literature that focuses on health care, education, and the human services.

The following list is not meant to be exhaustive but reflects some of the resources that I have found helpful in my training and consultation work. The annotations represent my views only, but I hope that they will provide the reader with a glimpse of what each resource has to offer.

ANNOTATED BIBLIOGRAPHY

Albin, J. M. (1992). *Quality improvement in employment and other human services*. Baltimore, MD: Paul H. Brookes.

One of the few specialized texts on Total Quality Management in the human services arena. Focuses on the application of quality techniques in rehabilitation and employment, but ideas can be applied to other human service settings.

Albrecht, K. (1988). *At America's service: How your company can join the customer service revolution*. New York: Warner Books.

A very readable primer on the art of "service management." Provides a good philosophical overview and practical step-by-step program for achieving service quality.

Albrecht, K. (1992). *The only thing that matters: Bringing the power of the customer into the center of your business*. New York: HarperBusiness.

An updated and expanded treatment of the basic service concepts presented in earlier works. Includes practical implementation ideas.

Albrecht, K., & Bradford, L. J. (1990). *The service advantage: How to identify and fulfill customer needs*. Homewood, IL: Dow Jones-Irwin.

A very good basic text on customers, how to identify their needs and develop customer report cards. Includes basic elements of survey research.

Barker, J. A. (1992). *Future edge: Discovering the new paradigms of success.* New York: William Morrow.

A thought-provoking and highly readable book about the power of paradigms and their implications for managing change and anticipating the future.

Berwick, D. M., Godfrey, A. B., & Roessner, J. (1991). *Curing health care: New strategies for quality improvement.* San Francisco: Jossey-Bass.

A report on the results of the National Demonstration Project (NDP) on Quality Improvement in Health Care. One of the earliest systematic studies in the health care arena. Describes the experiences of the health care organizations included in the study on applying TQM principles to achieve quality outcomes in health care.

Carr, D., & Littman, I. (1990). *Total Quality Management in the 1990's.* Arlington, VA: Coopers & Lybrand.

Application of TQM in the governmental sector (federal, state, and local). Good translation of concepts to public agencies. Helpful presentation of rationale for adoption of TQM principles by government.

Chang, R. Y. (1994). *Building a dynamic team: A practical guide to maximizing team performance.* Irvine, CA: Richard Chang Associates.

A basic handbook on team development and the various phases that teams go through as they grow and mature.

Chang, R. Y. (1994). *Success through teamwork: A practical guide to interpersonal team dynamics.* Irvine, CA: Richard Chang Associates.

A practical reference on team dynamics and how to effectively manage the team process for more successful outcomes.

Covey, S. R. (1990). *The seven habits of highly effective people: Restoring the character ethic.* New York: Simon & Schuster.

Still on the list of best-selling business books after several years, Covey's basic blueprint for improving personal effectiveness also provides a good base for improving organizational performance. Helpful perspective on countering learned helplessness in organizations through the practice of proactive behaviors.

Crosby, P. B. (1979). *Quality is free.* New York: Mentor.

Crosby's seminal work on the nature of quality, how to think about it, and how to achieve it. Provides a perspective from a manager turned teacher.

Deming, W. E. (1986). *Out of the crisis.* Cambridge: Massachusetts Institute of Technology, Center for Advanced Engineering Study.

Deming's basic work on Continuous Quality Improvement. Sometimes a bit "heavy," but definitely recommended for the serious student.

Harrington-Mackin, D. (1994). *The team building tool kit: Tips, tactics, and rules for effective workplace teams.* New York: American Management Association (AMACOM).

A comprehensive guide to the development and management of effective teams. Includes a description of various types of teams and how to handle difficult problems.

Jablonski, J. R. (1992). *Implementing TQM: Competing in the nineties through Total Quality Management.* San Diego: Pfeiffer & Company.

A very practical, step-by-step reference on the basics of TQM and how to implement a quality improvement process. Includes practical advice on forming a Quality Council and the use of process improvement teams.

Juran, J. (1989). *Juran on leadership for quality: An executive handbook.* New York: Free Press.

Juran's thoughts on quality including a discussion of his triad (quality planning, quality control, and quality improvement). Includes basic management strategies for implementing a performance improvement system.

Katzenbach, J. R., & Smith, D. K. (1993). *The wisdom of teams: Creating the high-performance organization.* New York: HarperBusiness.

A helpful guide to understanding teams and their potential, based on the authors' study of teams in a variety of organizations. Reviews basic elements of high-performance work teams. Includes a question-and-answer section on commonly asked questions about teams and team performance.

Kotter, J. P., & Heskett, J. L. (1992). *Corporate culture and performance.* New York: Free Press.

Report of the authors' research on the corporate culture and its impact on performance. Includes discussion of different cultural types and strategies on cultural change.

Leebov, W., & Ersoz, C. (1991). *The health care manager's guide to continuous quality improvement.* Chicago: American Hospital Publishing.

A practical application of quality management principles to the health care industry. Provides a good conceptual base and many practical exercises and tools.

Martin, L. L. (1993). *Total Quality Management in human service organizations.* Newbury Park, CA: Sage.

One of the few books available that discusses the application of the theories and techniques of Total Quality Management to the human services. A very readable introductory text.

Martin, L. L., & Kettner, P. M. (1996). *Measuring the performance of human service programs.* Thousand Oaks, CA: Sage.

A detailed and practical overview of how to improve the measurement of performance in the human services field. Provides a comprehensive framework of performance measurement, based on an integration of three basic perspectives: efficiency, effectiveness, and quality.

Neave, H. R. (1990). *The Deming dimension.* Knoxville, TN: SPC Press.

Provides a very readable overview of Deming's philosophy and theories. Written by an Englishman who has attended and assisted with numerous Deming seminars.

Sashkin, M., & Kiser, K. J. (1992). *Total quality management.* Seabrook, MD: Ducochon Press.

A very good primer on the whole area of quality management from the perspective of an organizational psychologist and a sociologist. A very good overview of philosophy, techniques, and tools in nontechnical language. Helpful emphasis on the importance of the organizational culture.

Scholtes, P. R. (1992). *The team handbook: How to use teams to improve quality.*

A popular book on the nuts and bolts of using teams to accomplish quality improvement objectives.

Senge, P. M. (1990). *The fifth discipline: The art and practice of the learning organization.* New York: Doubleday Currency.

A mind-expanding look at the concept of "systems thinking" and its impact on problem solving. Very helpful chapter on the importance of developing the organization's "governing ideas" (mission, vision, and values).

Sluyter, G. V., & Mukherjee, A. K. (1993). *Total Quality Management for mental health and mental retardation services: A paradigm for the '90s.* Annandale, VA: American Network of Community Options and Resources.

One of the first books to appear in the mental health literature on the application of quality management. Includes basic concepts and tools and discusses their application to mental health organizations. Includes a chapter on the use of control charting to improve clinical services in a mental health organization.

U.S. General Accounting Office. (1991). *Management practices: U.S. companies improve performance through quality efforts* (GAO/NSIAD- 91-190). Washington, DC: Author.

A good introduction to the essential elements of TQM and some preliminary research on its impact in the private sector. Copies may be obtained by calling the GAO at (202) 275-6241.

Walton, M. (1986). *The Deming management method.* New York: Perigee Books.

A highly readable overview of Deming's theories Recommended as a good introduction to Deming's work and quality management ideas.

Zeithaml, V. A., Parasuraman, A., & Berry, L. (1990). *Delivering quality service: Balancing customer perceptions and expectations.* New York: Free Press.

An empirically based study of service leadership. Excellent information on dimensions of customer satisfaction and tools for evaluating an organization's readiness for quality service. Includes a very helpful paradigm for explaining key elements of customer satisfaction.

Zemke, R., & Schaaf, D. (1989). *The service edge: 101 companies that profit from customer care.* New York: Plume.

A basic reference on service management. Outlines five important operating principles and profiles 101 successful service organizations.

VIDEOTAPES

I have found a number of videotapes helpful in my quality improvement training seminars. Here are some of my favorites.

The Deming Library. Films, Inc.
This is a 24-volume library that provides a thorough overview of the Deming philosophy and how it may be implemented. I sometimes use selected videos, especially Volume II, *The 14 Points,* for more advanced audiences, although it is fairly long for a video (40 minutes).

In Search of Excellence (Peters & Waterman). Video Arts, Inc.
A series of short vignettes about excellent U.S. companies. I particularly like the one on Disney World and use it often when helping organizations identify their customers and develop their governing ideas.

The Power of Vision (Joel Barker). Charthouse International Learning Corporation.
This is an inspirational look at the importance of setting a vision for the organization by futurist Joel Barker. I like to use it during strategic planning sessions and when developing governing ideas.

Excellence in the Public Sector (Tom Peters). Video Publishing House.
A well-done video by Tom Peters focusing on five organizations in the public or voluntary services sector that reflect performance excellence. Demonstrates the applicability of quality management principles to public sector organizations. The vignette about the juvenile detention center in New York City is excellent for discussing the organizational culture.

Tools for Continual Improvement. Executive Learning, Inc.
A five-film set that focuses on quality improvement team skills and various data-generating and analysis tools (e.g., brainstorming, cause-and-effect diagraming, flowcharting). The vignettes that demonstrate the various skills and tools are shown in an acute hospital setting. Sometimes I get mixed reviews from participants because of the rather stilted acting in the films, but the content is excellent. Other sets, demonstrating more advanced tools and techniques, are also available from Executive Learning, Inc.

Quality-Centered Management Video Series. Toastmasters International and Kantola Productions.
A four-film series focusing on various aspects of quality management (*Cornerstones of Quality, The Team Approach, Supervising for Quality,* and *The Customer Service Connection*). A very well done and relatively

inexpensive set of videos to help reinforce the message. Although the vignettes are done in manufacturing and sales settings, rather than in human services, the messages are easily transposable.

Quality in Behavioral Healthcare: A Changing Paradigm. Missouri Institute of Mental Health, St. Louis.

This is a 23-minute tape we made to provide a more tailored video for behavioral health care audiences. It includes a brief introduction to quality management, followed by a look at the application of quality ideas in a large public psychiatric hospital through the eyes of hospital staff involved in the process.

PERFORMANCE IMPROVEMENT TOOL KIT

The third set of resources in this chapter is a collection of selected quality improvement tools that are useful for performance improvement teams as they collect and analyze data to help them determine the root causes of organizational problems and to select alternative courses of action.

The tools selected are only a very small portion of all those available. One book I have includes more than 100 (Kanji & Asher, 1996)! Although improvements in manufacturing processes may indeed rely on a number of highly sophisticated analytical tools, such as control charting, human service organizations generally do not need a large selection. In my team leader/team facilitator training sessions, I focus on about 12 such quality tools, and they usually suffice for most problems. The reference list at the end of the chapter includes a number of sources for a more comprehensive listing.

In this section, I have listed those needed for the case study in Chapter 8, along with a couple of others helpful for generating ideas (brainstorming) and selecting alternatives (multivoting).

BRAINSTORMING GROUP TECHNIQUE

Brainstorming is a group technique that helps teams quickly generate, clarify, and evaluate a sizable list of ideas, problems, issues, or solutions. This technique is very useful in the identification of problem areas, possible causes of problems, and potential solutions.

There are two distinct and important phases in the brainstorming process: *idea generation* and *idea clarification*. To maximize the power of this technique, it is important that groups complete these two phases sequentially.

Phase 1. The team leader states the topic in specific terms and writes it on a flip chart. Also listed is the purpose of the brainstorming effort, for example, "To generate a list of potential causes of low morale."

- One or more recorders are selected to capture ideas on the flip chart. Two recorders can speed up the process by eliminating some down time between items.

- Each team member takes a turn, in sequence, continuing until all ideas are exhausted (10 to 15 minutes, depending on the number of team members). Members may pass a turn if no ideas come to mind.

Phase 2. The team reviews the list to clarify ideas and eliminate exact duplications (avoid the tendency to "clump" or "group" ideas at this point).

- The team leader calls out each idea in turn and the person who suggested the idea provides a brief explanation or clarification of the item. Team members may ask questions for clarification, but any further discussion of ideas is withheld until the team is satisfied that the list is complete and understood by all members.

- The team then decides on how the list will be used (e.g., selecting of a smaller number of ideas from the whole set, using an idea selection tool such as multivoting).

Some helpful guidelines for brainstorming follow:
- Before beginning, clearly state and agree on the purpose of the brainstorming effort.

- Each team member (including the recorder) should take a turn, in sequence, around the entire group, continuing until no new ideas are forthcoming. This puts people on alert and helps keep the flow of ideas going. Anyone may pass at any time.

- Present only one thought or idea at a time, and express it in a few words or phrases. This will help prevent "dissertations," especially because members know that they will have the opportunity to clarify later.

- Members should build on the ideas of others.

- Record ideas on a flip chart or use another method that makes them visible to all.

- Continue to push when ideas seem to slow down; often the best ones emerge then.

MULTIVOTING

Multivoting is a technique that helps the team narrow a longer list of ideas, often generated through brainstorming, to a smaller, more manageable list. This technique is also useful when the team is trying to determine which ideas are the most important or which should be kept for further consideration. Steps in the multivoting process follow:

1. Clarify the purpose of the multivoting technique—"What are we trying to accomplish?" Review the list of items generated through brainstorming and eliminate *exact duplicates*. Avoid the tendency to group or "clump" ideas at this point, as it may result in categories that are too broad to be useful. Assign a number to each of the remaining ideas on the list.

2. Establish a common and agreed-upon set of criteria to guide the multivoting process. The team lists those that seem the most relevant, such as, "When we vote we will be trying to identify ideas that meet these three criteria: (a) broadest impact on organizational performance, (b) within our control to accomplish, and (c) doable within a 1-year timetable."

3. Determine the number of voting points that will be allocated to each member for the multivoting process. A good guideline is to allocate about 25% of the total number of items on the list. For example, if the list contains 40 items, the team might want to allocate 10 votes to each team member.

4. Arrange the items sequentially on a flip chart, leaving about a 6-inch margin down the left side of the page. Give each member some type of materials for voting. I like to use stickers, tape, colored pens, or pieces of masking tape. If more than one flip chart page has been used, they should be placed side by side on the walls around the room.

5. Each member then comes up to the pages, looks over all the items, and places his or her ten markers in the margins of the ideas selected. Although there are variations on this theme, I generally suggest that members place only one vote per idea to avoid skewing the data.

6. After the voting has been completed, tally the votes for each item and arrange the items by order of points assigned. Then ask team members to review the items with the highest votes and decide where the cutoff should be for those to be included on the final list: those with eight or more votes? Five or more votes?

7. If the list is reduced to no more than seven or eight items, the group may wish to follow up with rank ordering if the number of items to be selected needs to be still smaller. Each member ranks the remaining items (1 = first choice, 2 = second, and so on). Ranks are then summed and displayed in descending order of choice, with the lowest scores indicating the most preferred.

8. One caution is in order: No method is foolproof. Even though multivoting is a good quantitative method for helping teams reach consensus on selection of ideas, members should not allow it to eliminate ideas about which one or more team members may feel very strongly. It is usually good to ask about strongly held ideas at the end of the process and keep those strongly held ideas. If a consensus does not emerge later on in the team process, they will be eliminated naturally.

TREND CHART

The trend chart (or run chart) is a line graph used to show measurements of a phenomenon over time. The trend chart is useful in identifying patterns in a data set. Examples include employee absenteeism by day for a month, medication errors for a unit, behavioral outbursts of a client, and number of telephone calls received. If a team were studying client injuries in a residential facility, a run chart might look like Figure 9.1.

Some helpful guidelines for preparing trend charts including the following:

1. Determine what is to be measured.
2. Establish equal interval time periods on the horizontal axis.
3. Determine an appropriate scale for the data set and place it on the vertical axis.
4. Place data points on the graph that correspond to the information collected and connect pairs of points with straight lines.
5. Label all parts of the chart clearly, including the date.
6. If multiple trends are to be shown (e.g., comparison data for all seven living units), be careful not to overclutter the chart.

THE PARETO CHART

The Pareto Chart is essentially a histogram in which the characteristics measured are ordered in decreasing frequencies to help identify those that account for most of the variance in the data (Pareto's 80/20 rule: 80% of the problems or results are traceable to 20% of the possible causes). Pareto

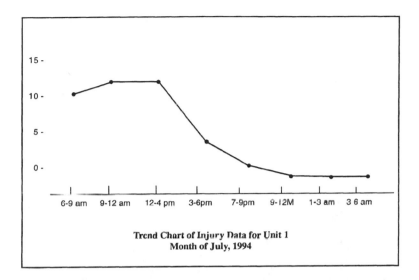

Figure 9.1. *Trend Chart of Injury Data for Unit 1, Month of July, 1994*

Charts help the team focus on those issues or causes that are the most critical to their analysis. Following is an example for a list of types of client injuries.

As shown in Figure 9.2, 70% of the major injuries at this facility fall into only two of the five categories listed. This information gives the team a good place to begin in deciding on specific areas for further investigation and analysis.

PROCESS FLOWCHART

A process flowchart is a visual representation of a process that shows the sequence of steps taken to complete a task or a sequence of operations in any process. Flowcharts are useful in helping a team understand a work process and how it can be improved. Flowcharts highlight areas in which inputs do not add value to the final output or outcome. Figure 9.3 is an example of a process flowchart of the admissions process for a community social service agency.

In this example, the team studying the admission process also added estimates of the average time it takes for an applicant to go through the process. With process charts like this, the team was able to identify aspects

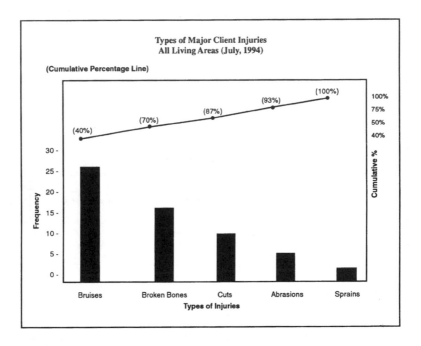

Figure 9.2. *Types of Major Client Injuries in All Living Areas (July, 1994)*

of the process that were causing delays and to make recommendations for improvements. The process flowchart is a useful tool whenever a team wants to understand a work process. It is a map of the steps for completing a task or job.

Suggested steps for developing process flowcharts including the following:

1. Identify the process to be charted (e.g., client admission process, procedure for reporting client injuries, travel voucher process, new employee application process).

2. Ask each team member to think about the steps in the process and write them down in a rough outline.

3. Based on team member input and using a flip chart, sketch out the major steps of the process using a block format. For example, if the team was looking at the employment process, it might begin with three major blocks of activities in the overall process: (a) recruiting, (b) interviewing, and (c) selecting. Each of these three blocks will have a number of steps that can be entered into the flowchart.

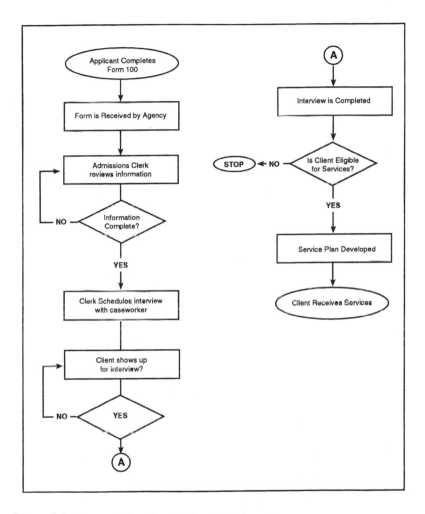

Figure 9.3. *Process Flowchart of the Admissions Process*

4. Steps that do not seem to fit logically at first may be placed to the side or in the "parking lot" for later consideration.
5. After reaching general consensus about the major steps or blocks, begin to refine the chart by using the standard flowchart symbols shown in Figure 9.4.
6. When finished, the team should "field test" the flowchart to see if it is accurate.

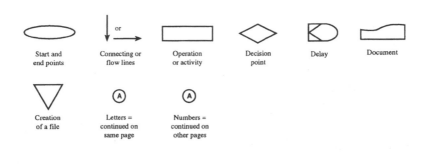

Figure 9.4. *Flowchart Symbols*

7. After verifying the chart, the team should examine the process to identify areas of duplication, rework, waste, or lack of value added. This analysis forms the basis for recommending and further testing changes to the process.

FISHBONE DIAGRAM

The fishbone diagram, also known as a "cause-and-effect" or Ishikawa Diagram, is useful in several phases of the performance improvement team process. At initial stages, it can help the team organize the results of brainstorming sessions into clusters of potential root causes of a quality problem. At later stages, it can be used to organize findings or surveys and other data collection efforts. An example of the basic diagram (without a complete listing of all the root causes) is shown in Figure 9.5.

The fishbone presents a visual description of the major groupings of causes for a quality problem. One approach is to use a standard set of categories for the main "bones" (e.g., environment, people, materials, policy, procedures, methods, machines). Another is to let the data suggest the major categories. In Figure 9.5, the data regarding the reasons for employee absenteeism loaded up along four major categories (supervision, weekend problems, professional support, and training).

The fishbone diagram in Figure 9.5 was developed by a team in the initial stages of root cause analysis through a brainstorming effort. It should not be verified through specific data collection efforts.

Steps in developing a fishbone diagram include the following:

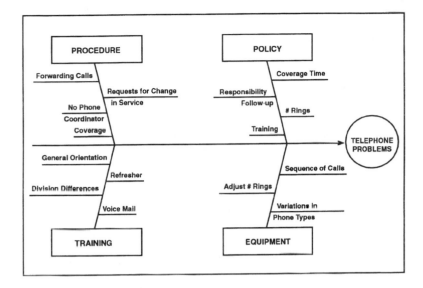

Figure 9.5. *A Fishbone Diagram*

1. Identify the problem to be addressed and write it in the head (box) of the diagram.

2. Begin working from the right to the left, identifying the major clusters of root causes that underlie the problem.

3. If using the fishbone at the early stages of the process, begin by brainstorming a list of possible causes of the problem.

4. Use a data refining process (e.g., affinity diagram) to cluster or group the ideas.

5. Begin with one major bone, such as "training" in the example.

6. For the first question (inadequate training for aides), ask, "How does this cause relate to the effect we are studying (absenteeism)?" When this has been answered, ask, "Why does this condition (inadequate training) exist?" Continue the process until the team can no longer identify root causes (answers to "why") or until the causes become obscure or too far removed from the team's span of influence.

7. After completing this process with the first question, repeat it for the second, and then for the rest of the major bones until no further causes can be identified. For causes that are unknown, write in "?" and note for a data collection effort.

8. Using the data generated, complete the fishbone for all clusters of major areas and root causes.

9. Examine the causes to identify areas needing more data and those over which the team is unlikely to have any control.

10. Begin a process of prioritizing the root causes that should be considered in developing recommendations for solutions.

REFERENCE MATERIALS USED FOR
THE PERFORMANCE IMPROVEMENT TOOL KIT

Kanji, G. K., & Asher, M. (1996). *100 methods for Total Quality Management.* Thousand Oaks, CA: Sage.

Leebov, W. (1991). *The quality quest: A briefing for health care professionals.* Chicago: American Hospital Publishing.

The memory jogger: A pocket guide of tools for continuous improvement. (1988). Methuen, MA: Goal/QPC.

A pocket guide to quality improvement tools. (1992). Oakbrook Terrace, IL: Joint Commission on Accreditation of Healthcare Organizations.

Sprint quality improvement process: Pocket guide. (1992). Spring and Qualtec.

Team meeting skills, group process skills guide and videotapes. (1992). Executive Learning, Inc.

Sluyter, G. V., & Mukherjee, A. K. (1993). *Total Quality Management for mental health and mental retardation services: A paradigm for the '90s.* Annandale, VA: American Network of Community Options and Resources.

INDEX

ABOUT THE AUTHOR

Gary V. Sluyter, PhD, MPH, is President of Development and Organizational Consultants, Inc., a firm in the St. Louis area specializing in training and development services for human service organizations. Dr. Sluyter has worked for the past 30 years as a clinician, administrator, researcher, and educator in a variety of service agencies, primarily in the field of mental health and mental retardation. He is former Director of the Mental Health Leadership Training Program with the Missouri Institute of Mental Health in St. Louis and previous Division Director for the Missouri Department of Mental Health. He also has held several academic appointments, including Associate Professor of Special Education Administration at Virginia Tech University and Clinical Associate Professor of Psychiatry, University of Missouri-Columbia. Dr. Sluyter's publications span 25 years and include more than 50 articles in professional journals, primarily in the areas of leadership, management, and organization systems. He is the author, with A. K. Mukherjee, of *Total Quality Management for Mental Health and Mental Retardation Services: A Paradigm for the '90s* (1993), the first text to systematically apply the theory and principles of Total Quality Management to the field of mental health. Dr. Sluyter's primary professional interests are in helping human service organizations improve their performance. His seminars on leadership and performance improvement have been widely attended by human services professionals.